When the World Closed Its Doors
Struggling to Escape Nazi-Occupied Europe

Ida Piller-Greenspan with Susan M. Branting

Routledge
Taylor & Francis Group

LONDON AND NEW YORK

First published 2006 by Paradigm Publishers

Published 2016 by Routledge
2 Park Square, Milton Park, Abingdon, Oxon OX14 4RN
711 Third Avenue, New York, NY 10017, USA

Routledge is an imprint of the Taylor & Francis Group, an informa business

Copyright © 2006 by Rosie Piller.

All rights reserved. No part of this book may be reprinted or reproduced or utilised in any form or by any electronic, mechanical, or other means, now known or hereafter invented, including photocopying and recording, or in any information storage or retrieval system, without permission in writing from the publishers.

Notice:
Product or corporate names may be trademarks or registered trademarks, and are used only for identification and explanation without intent to infringe.

Library of Congress Cataloging-in-Publication Data has been applied for.

Designed by Straight Creek Bookmakers

ISBN 13: 978-1-59451-253-7 (hbk)
ISBN 13: 978-1-59451-254-4 (pbk)

In loving memory of Morris Piller

Contents

List of prints	*ix*
Acknowledgments	*xiii*
Foreword	*xv*
Preface	*xxv*
1 We Dance at Our Wedding	*1*
2 Jolted Awake	*5*
3 Almost Arrested	*15*
4 Escape by Train	*25*
5 The Castle	*33*
6 Toward La Panne, near Dunkirk	*43*
7 Return to Antwerp	*57*
8 Surviving under the Nazis	*67*
9 Advice and Dissent	*75*
10 Unpleasant Surprises in Paris	*85*
11 Finding Shelter	*93*
12 Over the Mountains	*103*
13 Night in a Strange Hotel	*113*
14 Visa Maze	*121*
15 Escape	*131*
16 Hopes Dashed	*137*
17 The Train from Berlin	*147*
18 Reprieve	*155*
Afterword	*163*
Index	*169*
About the Author and Writer	*173*

Prints

1	Everyone rose to dance the *hora*.	2
2	We awoke in terror: Germany had invaded Belgium.	9
3	People hurried past, bug-eyed and surreal behind gas masks.	10
4	When we arrived at the station, all the trains were gone.	12
5	We hurried past jeering Belgians as German nationals were rounded up for deportation.	18
6	Suspected of being German parachutists, we were detained overnight in Brussels.	20
7	Our spirits rose as we boarded a train bound for the French border.	23
8	Nazi parachutists floated down like flowers around the train.	28
9	Before we reached Courtrai, the train jumped the tracks.	30
10	After 48 hours on the train, I was grateful for Red Cross coffee.	32
11	We found lodging in a small castle.	36
12	The train station was destroyed and all our luggage lost.	38
13	Barbed wire and determined guards stopped us at the French border.	41
14	German planes strafed fleeing refugees on the road to the coast.	46
15	A woman wailed for help for her dead child.	47
16	We found shelter in a basement in La Panne, near Dunkirk.	49

17	Every kind of vessel was put to use by people desperate to cross the English Channel.	51
18	A hellish light from incendiary bombs lit the town at night.	52
19	The beach was littered with the bodies of dead English soldiers.	53
20	German soldiers biked into La Panne to tell us we were "saved."	54
21	Turned away at the French border, we made our way back to Antwerp.	61
22	My parents were gone, and their store and home had been ransacked.	65
23	Unemployed Belgians signed up for work in Germany.	71
24	German troops sang as they marched through the streets.	72
25	I hugged my mother goodbye, wondering if I would ever see her again.	79
26	While hitchhiking, we were picked up by German military trucks.	81
27	Paris had fallen and refugees were being turned away. How would we get through?	88
28	The Germans were everywhere, but Maurice and I lingered to see the sights.	90
29	We found refuge in a barn as we fled to Bordeaux.	96
30	The hotel lobby was filled with sleeping refugees.	98
31	We surveyed the Cirque de Gavarnie before setting out to cross the Pyrenees.	101
32	We started our exhausting climb before dawn.	107
33	The Spanish patrol forced us back across the border.	111
34	We pleaded with the refugees not to return to Belgium.	118
35	We slept in an abandoned tunnel with other refugees.	124
36	In Marseilles, we waited 48 hours for each of our visas.	126
37	Our hearts leapt as we crossed the border into Spain.	129

38	In Barcelona, a local Jewish organization gave us shelter.	*134*
39	At last we arrived in Lisbon.	*140*
40	Jewish refugees crowded the soup kitchen.	*142*
41	Nowhere to go—the world had closed its doors.	*146*
42	The sealed train opened, and hundreds of Berlin Jews poured out.	*150*
43	I wept as the men, women, and children were forced back onto the train.	*152*
44	In desperation, we signed up to drain the swamps in the Dominican Republic.	*158*
45	We left for New York on the SS *Nyassa*.	*160*

Acknowledgments

My name is Rosie Piller, and I have been intimately involved in bringing the artwork and story of my mother, Ida Piller-Greenspan, to publication. I have many people to thank for making this book possible.

First, I am grateful to my mother for being willing to return to her darkest memories in order to leave a legacy for her grandchildren.

I would like to thank Susan M. Branting for her patience and expertise in writing a page-turning narrative that remains true to my parents' story and captures the grief, uncertainty, and terror they endured.

I am indebted to Dean Birkenkamp of Paradigm Publishers for suggesting, on a hike years ago after seeing my mother's exhibit and hearing her talk, that I should seriously consider publishing her artwork and story because they were so haunting. Many thanks to Jason Potter for designing the book and for his advice and support in creating high-resolution scans of the prints. Todd Lape designed the striking book cover using one of my mother's prints, and George Zirfas created the maps showing my parents' itinerary. I am grateful to Peter Rose for writing the Foreword, and to Leslie Lomas for helping to arrange that. Many thanks to Alison Sullenberger, who so capably handled the marketing of this book, and to the rest of the staff at Paradigm Publishers for all their support.

Rosemary Carstens helped us by writing a heartfelt book proposal that caught the eye of several publishers. My son Robert Piller typed up the original version of his grandmother's story and scanned the prints into digital files so we could include them in the book proposal. Jody Berman gave me excellent advice on what factors make this book unique, how to look for publishers and agents, and how to evaluate various offers. Debra Halperin Biasca edited the manuscript and was very supportive throughout the process.

Thanks to my first cousins Marc Dorian and Charly Szwajcer, who lived through the war and helped us fill in some of the gaps in the story.

Last but certainly not least, I would like to thank my loving parents, Morris and Ida, for setting their grief and anger aside and bringing us up on the Golden Rule. My sister Liane and I learned about the Holocaust at an early age and, thankfully, the focus was not on hatred but on the lessons to be learned regarding resistance to oppression and compassion for the oppressed.

Rosie Piller
Boulder, Colorado
January 2006

Foreword

Adolf Hitler's Mein Kampf, published in 1924, first outlined a political philosophy and scheme for a new Teutonic state based on a combination of blood, soil, and national socialism. Filled with passion, pomposity, and paranoia, it was studded with heroic figures and villainous ogres, the worst of them all being "the parasitic Jew." In the key chapter on "Nation and Race," Hitler stated that, among all peoples, the Jew represented the mightiest antithesis to the "noble Aryan." In a classic example of scapegoating, he claimed that Jews were responsible for all the ills of modern society: capitalism and communism; clannishness and internationalism; decadent art and decadent science. He threatened to purge the system of those he called "Germany's misfortune."

Within a decade, Hitler rose from relative obscurity to become Chancellor and Führer, the supreme ruler of Germany, and he began to implement his plan. He claimed that his master-race Aryans were the fittest and noblest and most deserving of ruling the world, and to insure their superior place in his new order, he augmented this doctrine with a eugenics scheme that led to one of the most heinous examples of social engineering in history. He convinced his followers that the Jews were Untermenschen (subhuman) and, once he assumed power, treated them as if they were vermin to be trapped and exterminated.

Anti-Semitism was hardly a new phenomenon. Hostility to Jews was known in Roman times and in the early Christian period. Gospel writers accused Jews of deicide, the killing of Jesus, and for centuries such charges were a standard element of church teachings.

In the early days of the Crusades, Jews were butchered in parts of what is now Germany, and many who survived fled to Eastern Europe. In the medieval period and well into the Renaissance, Jews were often confined to certain areas or ghettos, forbidden to own property or work the soil, and consigned to particular middleman occupations, such as money-lending, leading to the widely exploited stereotype of Jews as usurers.

In 1492, the Spanish rulers Ferdinand and Isabella imposed their Inquisition, forcing Spanish Jews to convert to Catholicism or move to other parts of the Spanish Empire. Some fled to other Mediterranean countries, South America, and the Caribbean.

Martin Luther had thought Jews would rally to his protests against the Roman Catholic Church, but once he found they were not about to abandon their religious beliefs, he turned against them. Many of his followers followed suit.

In Czarist Russia in the late nineteenth century, charges of "blood libel," the killing of Christian babies for ritual purposes, were leveled at Jews. The government often abetted these fantastic accusations, using them as excuses for sanctioned pogroms, which were organized campaigns of harassment that often resulted in the burning and looting of Jewish homes and synagogues. Attacks, threats, and the drafting of Jewish men for long terms in the army were largely responsible for several million East European Jews emigrating to the United States, which, at the time, still had an open door for European émigrés.

During the same period, Jews in Western Europe also had to contend with deeply rooted prejudices, and many suffered from unjust persecution. Yet for all this anti-Semitism, explicitly "racial" arguments were rarely used. Some of Hitler's ideas had their roots in the writings of the American physician, eugenicist, and ecologist Madison Grant. In his best-known work, *The Passing of the Great Race*, published in 1915, Grant wrote that the United States, a society in which institutionalized racism against Americans from Africa was already well known, was being inundated by "the weak, broken and mentally crippled of all races drawn from the lowest stratum of the Mediterranean basin and the Balkans, together with hordes of wretched, submerged populations of the Polish ghettos." The last reference was clearly about Jews. Grant offered a variety of ways of coping with those "undesirable people" who had already "infected" society, including the use of compulsory sterilization and euthanasia.

Grant's racial theories were widely discussed in the United States, and some were used to restrict the influx of such "inferior" beings culminating in the immigration restriction laws of 1921 and 1924. However, it was in Hitler's Germany that racial discrimination against Jews was first implemented on a grand scale. (Hitler was a great admirer of Grant and had his book translated and distributed throughout his new domain.)

In 1933, with the German economy in shambles and with many parties vying for seats in the Reichstag, Hitler's National Socialist (Nazi) Party took control of the government. His first acts included starting a massive program of rearmament and formulating a blueprint for the establishment of a "Thousand Year Reich" that included implementing what would eventually become known as "The Final Solution," the plan to rid Germany and then the world of the "perfidious Jews."

Hitler's new Reich would last only twelve years. But during that period, the Germans rearmed their country, rebuilt the economy, occupied much of Europe, provoked, fought, and then lost one of the bloodiest and most costly wars in history, and almost carried out their *Führer*'s maniacal scheme to make the world Judenfrei (free of Jews). By the time of his death by suicide in a Berlin bunker in April of 1945, a month before Germany's collapse and unconditional surrender to the Allied Forces, the European continent was in ruin. An estimated twenty million people had died in the conflict, including six million Jewish men, women, and children who had been starved in ghettos or concentration camps or murdered by firing squads or in gas chambers.

In the beginning, Hitler's minions, abetted by an amazingly compliant citizenry, first sought to expropriate Jewish properties, then tried to force the Jews out of the country and to control those who remained. Using Jim Crow rules of segregation in the

American south as a model, Hitler, on September 10, 1935, implemented what came to be known as the Nuremburg Laws on Blood and Race. These laws spelled out the requirements of citizenship in the Third Reich, assuring "the purity of German blood and German honor" and clarifying the position of Jews in the Reich. Article 4 explicitly stated, "A Jew cannot be a citizen of the Reich. He cannot exercise the right to vote; he cannot hold public office." The following article indicated precisely who fell under such restrictions and the "racial bases" of this pattern of discrimination in the early days of the Third Reich.

> ARTICLE 5
> (1) A Jew is an individual who is descended from at least three grandparents who were, racially, full Jews.
> (2) A Jew is also an individual who is descended from two full-Jewish grandparents if:
> > (a) he was a member of the Jewish religious community when this law was issued, or joined the community later;
> > (b) when the law was issued, he was married to a person who was a Jew, or was subsequently married to a Jew;
> > (c) he is the issue from a marriage with a Jew, in the sense of Section I, which was contracted after the coming into effect of the Law for the Protection of German Blood and Honor of September 15, 1935;
> > (d) he is the issue of an extramarital relationship with a Jew ... and was born out of wedlock after July 31, 1936.

Later, these draconian definitions were made more comprehensive to include many who were even more marginally Jewish.

In addition to stripping Jews of their livelihood, the right to attend public schools and universities or to practice their professions, the Nazis denied them access to public transport, libraries and other facilities, and humiliated them at every turn. Sometimes accusations of being in league with the hated Communists and charges of disloyalty (even directed at medal-bearing German Jewish veterans of World War I) were added to the racist arguments.

In November 1938, the first major coordinated campaign of outright violence occurred. It came to be known as *Kristallnacht*, "The Night of Broken Glass," when rampaging mobs attacked Jewish shops, homes, and synagogues, as well as people. They knew whom to go after: swastika-bearing brown-shirted bullies, their superiors, and sympathizers had painted the six-pointed Star of David on Jewish-owned properties. Soon the Party would require all Jews to wear large yellow stars with the word "Jude" in bold letters on their outer garments and to have their identity papers stamped with a "J."

While the noose was tightening around the Jews, the Nazis were on the move in their campaign for *Lebensraum* (literally, living space, but really a euphemism for territorial conquest and world domination). In 1938, German troops rolled triumphantly into Austria, Hitler's country of birth. Many Austrians welcomed this *Anschluss* (annexation) and greeted the Germans as heroes. In all of the other lands, the reception of the conquerors was far less benign, although in most cases capitulation was more common than resistance. In a short period, the German armies overran Poland, Czechoslovakia, and other lands to the east, and occupied Denmark and Norway as well as France, Belgium, and The Netherlands. In each country, the Nazis installed puppet regimes to run their affairs and carry out their orders, including "Jewish racial laws" like those in Germany. This included the requirement to wear the stigmatizing yellow stars, often marked with the word "Jew" written in the local language ("Juif" in France, "Jood" in The Netherlands and the Flemish parts of Belgium). Jews were stripped of their possessions and taken to holding centers to be deported to concentration camps or segregated into ghettoes from which they would later be transported to camps in Germany and Austria and in many other countries. The names of those places live in infamy: Dachau, Matthausen, Westerbork, Theresienstadt, Bergen-Belsen, Auschwitz-Birkenau, and hundreds more. Many prisoners were killed immediately, while others were used as slave laborers and were later exterminated.

There is ample evidence that during this period there was a growing awareness not only on the Continent but also in the United

States of what was happening to European Jewry. Leaders in those countries as yet untouched by the Nazis might have provided safe havens for those fortunate enough to either escape ahead of the Nazis or after an invasion, but did very little. Some, indeed many, were hostile to pleas for assistance or asylum, even though the violence of *Kristallnacht* had been widely reported.

With bitter sarcasm, Chaim Weizmann, Israel's first president, would later describe the western world of the 1930s as "divided into two parts—those places where the Jews could not live and those they could not enter."

When the Canadian foreign minister was asked how many Jewish refugees his country might absorb, he tersely stated, "None is too many."

Those few who managed to get to Australia were put into detention centers; they were seen as security risks because, ironically, of their German citizenship.

And the United States, whose iconic Statue of Liberty welcomes those "yearning to breathe free," was hardly better. In fact, owing to both the restrictive immigration rules of the 1920s, which had reduced the number of visas to a bare minimum, and widespread anti-foreign and anti-Semitic sentiment across the United States, and especially within President Franklin Delano Roosevelt's State Department, almost nothing was done. And this remained the case even when it was clear that genocide was taking place. As historian David Wyman and others have noted, the barriers were of paper, but they were as high and protective as if they had been made of barbed wire.

At one point there seemed to be chance for a breakthrough and an opportunity to change restrictive policies. Under pressure to do something about the fact that hundreds of thousands of Jews in Germany and Austria were desperately seeking asylum, President Roosevelt called a conference to discuss the plight of refugees. Roosevelt himself did not attend, nor did his Secretary of State or Attorney General, the heads of the only departments that could make exceptions to the stringent visa restrictions.

Roosevelt sent a much lower level representative to the gathering held in the resort city of Evian, France.

During nine days in July 1938, delegates from thirty-two countries expressed great concern, but, beyond verbal hand wringing, nothing was done. And, despite the rapid escalation of atrocities, they never met again.

Many have argued that the United States and other western countries, still in the throes of the Great Depression, feared that granting asylum would increase labor unrest as the refugees competed with citizens for jobs and would strain overburdened and under-funded welfare services. Others, especially those known as isolationists, feared that acquiescing to such demands could be construed as a signal that America would be getting more deeply involved in a foreign conflict they were seeking so assiduously to avoid. Still others contended (often behind the scenes and within the administration itself) that the biggest problem with the asylum-seekers was that most were Jews, and in the climate of widespread domestic anti-Semitism, they were particularly sensitive to charges that, already captive of "Jewish interests," they were being used once again.

In the end, as one person reported, "Delegate after delegate rose to express sympathy for the refugees. But most countries, including the United States and Britain, offered excuses for not letting in more refugees. Even efforts by some Americans to rescue children failed." In the United States, the Wagner-Rogers bill, an effort to admit 20,000 endangered Jewish refugee children, was rejected by the Senate in 1939 and again in 1940.

While the barriers to asylum were being reinforced, more and more European Jews were being rounded up. Bewildered, frightened, and increasingly alert to what was happening to those already deported, their sense of despair escalated. Some resigned themselves to the fate that would eventually become the rule for the overwhelming majority of Jews. Some joined partisan groups trying to create an insurgency against the Nazis. Others fought back in several memorable ghetto uprisings.

There were those—my Dutch wife, Hedy Cohen, and her sister, Betsy, among them—who were fortunate to find courageous Christians willing to risk everything to hide them in a cellar or attic; others had special friends who spirited them or their children out of the cities to the countryside. And some Jews, like Ida and Maurice Piller, the principal actors in the remarkable narrative that follows, decided to take their chances by keeping one step ahead of the authorities in the conviction that somehow they would be saved. Unfortunately, only a few of the resisters, the hidden children, or those who tried to flee succeeded in eluding their hunters, and most ended up suffering the same dire destiny of those they had left behind.

The experiences of these people have been reconstructed and analyzed by historians and social scientists who have examined millions of documents, conducted thousands of interviews, and read hundreds of eye-witness accounts written during the war (such as Anne Frank's diary) or immediately thereafter (like that of Primo Levi), and, more recently, recounted in memoirs of those who experienced the atrocities and lived to tell about their small part in the overall catastrophe. Some of the latter books have been published, often privately, years—even decades—after the events described.

Such reminiscences are fraught with problems, for they are recollections of events long ago and, almost by necessity, reconstructions of them. Yet, the horrors of the Holocaust have been etched so profoundly on those who endured them that the core elements must surely reflect the critical essence of what really happened. Such works put flesh on the bare bones of history and on the dry calculus of the annihilation. The works of the survivors remind us that every single one of the six million victims was not a statistic but a living, breathing, complex, and unique human being, filled with hopes and fears, joys and sorrows, pleasures and pains, and a myriad of personal experiences.

There are quite a number of such accounts available for those interested. Some are highly literary; many are rather pedestrian; but all are evocative—and troubling. They force their readers to ask, "How could this be?" "How could human beings do what was done to these people?" "Why did so few offer protection, comfort, and solace?" "Why didn't sovereign nations professing to be democratic bastions open their gates more than a tiny crack?" "Can it happen again?"

These are surely the questions the Polish-born, Belgian-raised artist, refugee, and long-time American citizen Ida Piller-Greenspan must have asked herself time and again over the past sixty-five years.

When the World Closed Its Doors is Ida's story and that of her husband, Maurice.

In the pages that follow, we are told that Ida and Maurice were married in the Belgian city of Antwerp on the evening of May 9, 1940. At 4:30 the next morning, their world turned topsy-turvy as they and their families faced the reality of the German invasion. As readers, we become secret travelers with the fleeing couple, witnessing their entire ordeal. Their mid-twentieth century odyssey, described here through the close collaboration of Ida and her chronicler, Susan M. Branting, is a dramatic account of the experiences of two people caught in the maelstrom of history, trying to avoid being yet two more hapless victims in the tragedy that would come to be summarized in a single word: Auschwitz.

Reading about the Pillers' tribulations and studying Ida's haunting monoprints, we are caught up in issues that transcend their particular plight: the fragmentation of the family, the wrenching losses that ensue, and, above all, what it must have felt like to be abandoned by the world. When we put the book down, we realize that we have been given more than a glimpse of what it means to be uprooted, homeless, and countryless, too.

Ida and Maurice were two of millions. Their story is at once unique and universal. In many ways, their voices speak for a multitude of the dispossessed that Adolf Hitler was intent on destroying.

Peter I. Rose

Peter Rose, a sociologist and writer, is Sophia Smith Professor Emeritus at Smith College. His recent books include *Tempest-Tost*, *The Dispossessed*, *They and We*, 6th edition, and a memoir, *Guest Appearances and Other Travels in Time and Space*.

Preface

When memories are edged with fear and grief, it is often best to put them aside, to speak of them as little as possible. That is what Ida Piller-Greenspan did for forty years with her memories of escaping from Europe at the beginning of World War II when Jews were hunted and much of the world refused to take them in.

In those forty years, she raised two daughters, lost her first love, and married a second husband. In those forty years, she used her art to explore the world rather than to turn an inward eye upon her past.

In the late 1970s, when Ida's daughter Rosie became pregnant with Ida's first grandchild, Ida was suddenly filled with a desire to leave a testament to her experiences. This desire brought a flood of images to her dreams and waking life. An accomplished artist, Ida chose to communicate those memories through art, specifically through the dream-like quality of monoprints. She also wrote a brief summary of the events, to accompany the monoprints.

Monoprints are created by pressing paper onto an inked plate made of plastic or metal. The artist inks the entire plate with a roller, then wipes away areas that she wants to appear white. Thus, she is drawing in reverse, as if she were painting a negative of the scene she wants to depict. The artist then places paper on the plate and rolls it through a printing press. When the paper is pulled off the plate, all of the ink comes with it—there is no ink left on the plate for a second print. Because each monoprint is a singular piece of art that cannot be replicated, it is as unique and fragile as Ida's memories.

Ida's survival in the face of incredible odds was not typical of Jews in Europe at that time. Of the nine million Jews living in Europe at the beginning of World War II, two thirds were gassed in concentration camps or shot in dark forests above hastily dug pits, or they wasted away from disease and starvation in overcrowded ghettos. Many of the remaining third hid, while a few were whisked away by sympathetic countrymen. Only a small percentage of refugees were granted visas by other countries willing to take them in.

In the United States, immigration was restricted by quotas based on nationality rather than need. By 1939, the United States was admitting only 154,000 immigrants annually, and 84,000 of those had to be British or Irish. Unemployment, anti-Semitism, an attitude of America for Americans, and a suspicion that some immigrants might be saboteurs or spies kept out refugees like Ida and her husband Maurice.

Other countries set their own quotas and restrictions for their own reasons. Britain wanted to avoid an influx of Jews to Palestine. Cuba required immigrants to have $3,000 each, a fortune in those years following the worldwide Great Depression. Spain, still reeling from a devastating civil war, wanted nothing to do with the refugee "problem." Even when a country cracked open its doors to let in a few, refugees were often at the mercy of diplomats who had no sympathy for their plight. While a few ambassadors and consuls bent the law, most did not. Whatever their reasons, too many countries closed their doors to the Jews and others fleeing the Nazis. In the end, the smattering of people who survived did so through perseverance, courage, and the whims of fortune.

This is Ida's story of just such ingenuity and luck, as told in the pictures she created. The words that accompany the monoprints capture the essence of her tale. It is a story filled with harrowing experiences of fear, sleep deprivation, hunger, and shock, and sometimes with laughter. And though Ida and Maurice escaped with their lives, they did not escape from the painful memories of what happened to those they left behind.

Now, imagine Ida Piller-Greenspan sixty years ago. Her face is round beneath a blonde pageboy. People tease her about her hooded eyes. "Bette Davis eyes," they say. Her figure is sturdy and muscular, as befits a champion swimmer. She is almost twenty-one years old and is about to marry the darkly handsome Maurice Piller.

Ida and Maurice Piller on their wedding day, May 9, 1940.

1

We Dance at Our Wedding

1. Everyone rose to dance the hora.

Maurice picked up his foot and brought it down sharply on the bundle on the floor, an empty wine glass wrapped in a napkin.

—*Mazel Tov! Mazel Tov!* Good luck! Congratulations!

The cry rose from some of the two hundred guests that filled the synagogue.

Maurice looked up, his deep-brown eyes smiling into mine. We had wanted to marry a year ago, and the joy we felt now as we finally stood together beneath the *huppah* must have made us glow. It was the happiest moment of my life.

The *huppah*, a canopy draped on four poles, was a Jewish symbol for our first home. The breaking of the glass was symbolic, too, a reminder of the fragility both of relationships and of a world filled with suffering, even as we celebrated. But Maurice and I were oblivious to anything but our love on that cool May afternoon in 1940 in Antwerp, Belgium.

Later that evening the twenty people who were dearest to me and my new husband gathered in a rented room to celebrate our wedding. We talked and joked, and when someone turned up the phonograph, we jumped up and danced the *hora*, linking arms and kicking our feet. Around and around we flung ourselves. Around and around until we collapsed exhausted into chairs, panting and laughing.

I wish I could remember every moment of that evening: the play of light on beloved faces, the sound of merry voices—my dear friends Paula and Rachel, my mother, my father, my sisters Rosa and Annie, Annie's husband Max, their little towheaded son Charly, Maurice's parents, Leon and Rudel, Maurice's sisters Cylia and Bronia, Bronia's teenage son Marc, and Maurice's friends—so many people, too many of them gone. How could I know that this would be the last time I would ever see some of them? How could I know that among those I would lose forever were my mother, my father, and my dear sister Roseke?

It was May 9, 1940. I was beginning a new chapter in my life. I thought I knew what lay ahead, but in less than twelve hours,

Maurice and I would embark on a journey that would ultimately determine whether we lived or died.

2

Jolted Awake

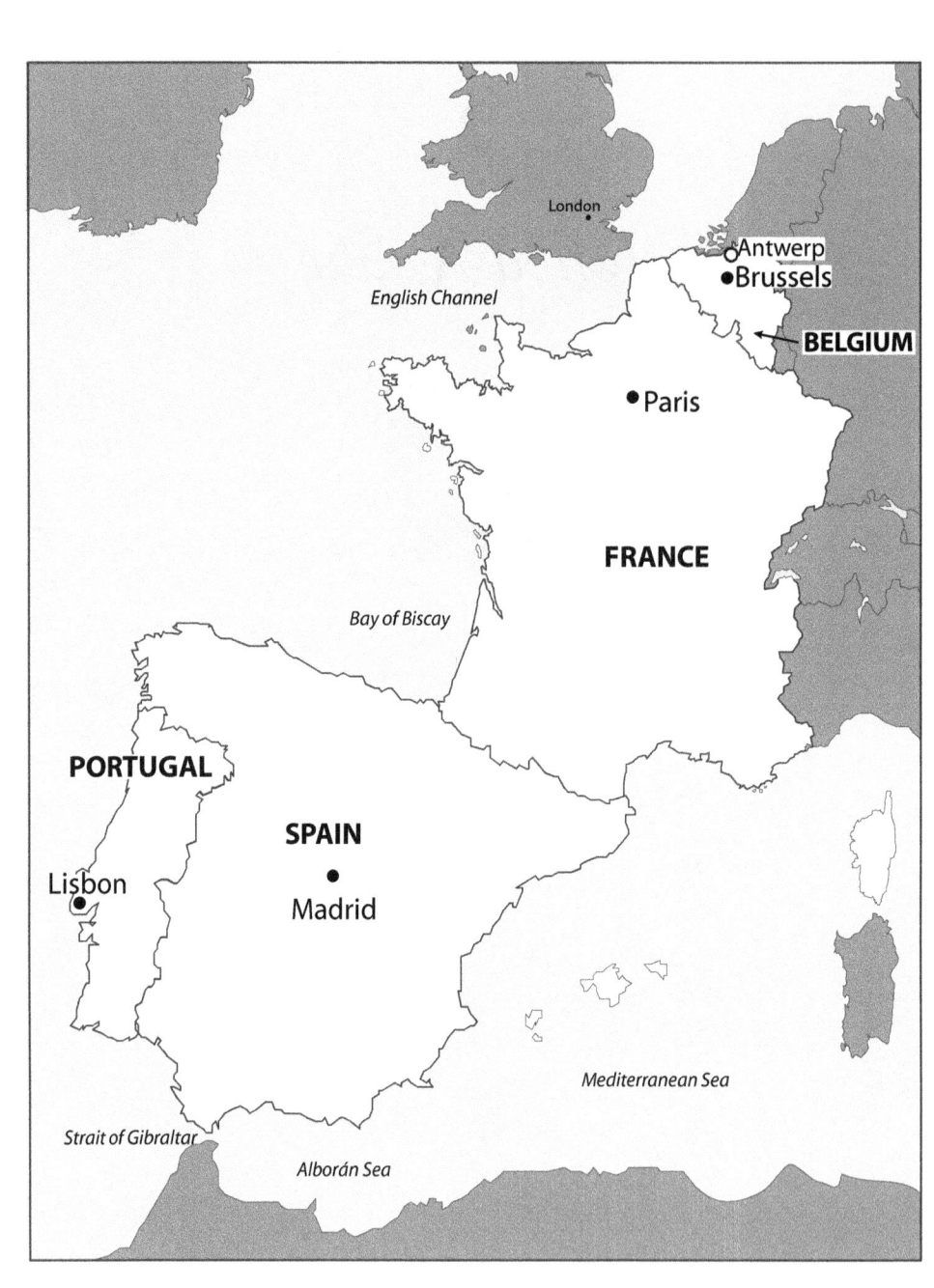

Maurice set down our small valises on the train platform and took off his fedora. With his full lips and thick lashes, he was, I thought, the handsomest man in the world.

He ran a hand through his hair, resettled his hat, smiled at me, then called in French to a railway employee.

—Can you direct us to the train to Ostend?

—You've got to go to the South Station, *Monsieur*. But I don't think you can make it now. That train is leaving in fifteen minutes.

Maurice and I looked at each other in disappointment. We had left our wedding reception in Antwerp two hours ago, changed into traveling clothes, and caught a train to Brussels. Here we had intended to connect to a train to Ostend, a resort city on the Belgian coast, for our honeymoon. We had arrived in the North Station, not realizing that the Ostend train left from the South Station.

I sighed, the excitement of the day weighing on my shoulders.

—I'm tired, Maurice.

—Is there a hotel around here?

—*Oui*. Down this street my cousin has a little hotel. The price is good, and it's quiet.

Maurice put his arm around me and led us out of the station and into the lights of the city. The sky was dark and clear, the thinnest sliver of a moon drifting in and out of high wispy clouds. It had been an unusually dry May, and the night was beautiful.

* * *

We woke wide-eyed, the shock and *thud-thud!* of anti-aircraft fire bringing us up sharply from dreamless sleep.

—What...?

—It must be the army, practicing.

—It's so close!

—What time is it?

—4:30.

The Belgium military periodically conducted military maneuvers, firing its anti-aircraft guns. There was also the occasional skirmish with German aircraft. We had come to expect it, but this was all wrong—too close, too loud.

My pulse pounded in my throat. I put a hand to my heart to calm it.

The reverberations continued, and now I heard the distant whine of an airplane engine. I threw off the quilt and hurried to the window, drawing aside the curtain.

Outside, sparks of light flickered off high clouds. The engine's whine, the persistent *thud-thud!*—it all increased as I watched. Then I heard a strange scream, an inhuman shriek from the sky that turned my blood to ice.

Maurice had come to stand beside me. Now he pulled on his pants and left the room. A minute later he was back. I turned to see him standing in the doorway, backlit by a hall light, his face in darkness. He moved as if to speak, but he was interrupted by the distorted squawk of a radio announcer blaring from the hotel lobby down the hall.

—*We are under attack! The Germans have invaded! They have broken through the Maginot Line! France, Belgium, and Holland are under attack! We are pleading for the help of our English friends!*

Again, the shriek. In an instant, Maurice was by my side, staring at the sky. The shriek, then *thud-thud!*

—Those are *Stukas*. German bombers. Their sirens sound as they dive. It's meant to scare you.

—We have to get back to Antwerp, to our families!

The thought of a German invasion was terrifying. We had heard too many stories of how the Germans treated their own Jews—thrown out of jobs and homes, beaten, forced to flee without a *pfennig* in their pockets—to be naïve about what would be in store for us if they should succeed in their invasion.

We threw our clothes into our valises and raced through the lobby, now filled with milling guests with pale, stricken faces. Maurice paused to call his fourteen-year-old nephew Marc who

2. We awoke in terror: Germany had invaded Belgium.

3. People hurried past, bug-eyed and surreal behind gas masks.

had come to the wedding and had gone home to Brussels on his own because he had school the next day. Marc told Maurice that his mother, Bronia, had called and told him to wait for her. His father was in Palestine; there had been a divorce when Marc was six.

Outside, the street was busy with people hurrying in the strange half-light of predawn, their faces bug-eyed and surreal behind gas masks. Three months before, when Germany had invaded Norway, the Belgium government, fearing a replay of the gas attacks of World War I, had issued gas masks to everyone. Of course, Maurice and I had left ours in Antwerp. One more thing to make us tense.

As we neared the train station, the crowds thickened and moved with more purpose. At the station we discovered that the trains heading north to Antwerp had already gone.

We waited impatiently, setting down our valises and pacing or shifting from foot to foot, unable to calm our anxiety. Finally, a station employee announced that the trains were running again, but we discovered that the tickets had all been sold. We continued our wait, listening all the while to the distant sounds of war creeping closer and closer.

At last a train arrived that could take us. We squeezed onto it and sat on our valises amid the smells and screams of babies, the disturbing questions of white-faced children, and the quiet sobs and angry voices of frightened people. Belgian soldiers in khaki uniforms slouched against the train's walls, their rifles slung over their shoulders, their faces pensive as they stared out the windows.

In Antwerp, the same mayhem and fear pervaded the station and streets. My parents lived in a two-story house on Omegangstraat, above the shop where my father worked fourteen-hour days selling upholstery and drapery fabric, stuffing for furniture and mattresses, thread, and numerous other notions of the decorating trade. We rushed to my parents' home. It was locked, but I had a key. We climbed the stairs, our hearts pounding.

—Mama! Papa!
—Where could they be?

4. When we arrived at the station, all the trains were gone.

I ran into their bedroom and looked under the bed. Their valises were missing. They must have already gone. But where? They might have gone looking for us in Ostend, or perhaps they left to seek safety in France...?

We ran back down the stairs and out into the street. The trams were traveling their routes as usual, as if the whole world had not suddenly been turned on its head. We caught a tram to the home of Maurice's parents.

Maurice paused outside the door, took a deep breath, then turned the knob.

His father, Leon Piller, an elderly and deeply religious man with a full salt-and-pepper beard sat at the dining table, his hands around a cup of coffee growing cold. His head was cocked toward a noisy radio in the corner.

—We have to leave, Papa. We have to get out.

Maurice's mother appeared in the doorway to their bedroom, a blouse draped over her arm. A thin woman, she wore her hair cropped short and covered with a *scheitel*, a wig traditionally worn by married Jewish women. She had borne nine children, but only five had lived past childhood.

—I told him. We have to get out of here. Cylia's in the basement.

—The basement?

—Burning papers.

Cylia, like her sister Bronia—Marc's mother—had worked for an anti-Nazi group. The papers she was burning would be dangerous in the wrong hands. It was a good guess that Bronia was destroying papers in Brussels, too.

Maurice's father listened as the words danced around him. Maurice's father and mother were in their seventies, so there was good reason for Leon's hesitancy in undertaking such a journey. (Maurice was about to turn thirty-one; he was the youngest in the family.) Finally, though, his father nodded and stood up.

—We have to go to Brussels first. We must get Bronia and Marc.

I heard Maurice exhale audibly. We would go to France.

Germany was on the move again, hungry for revenge after the humiliation of the First World War, ravenous for land to expand its borders. By the summer of 1939, Germany had annexed Austria and invaded Czechoslovakia, Poland, Denmark and Norway. The Blitzkrieg—the lightning war in which Hitler launched his enormous military ground and air resources against Belgium, Holland, Luxembourg and France—should have been expected. But those countries did not expect German military might to roll through the rough terrain of the Ardennes Mountains in Belgium and Luxembourg, or to circumvent the string of French fortresses known as the Maginot Line (to which the English had contributed men and armaments). Europe was once again in turmoil, and people began to flee. Among those fleeing were thousands of Jews who were well aware of Hitler's anti-Semitic sentiments. Many of them, including Ida's family, had housed Jews fleeing Germany after Hitler became the German chancellor in 1933.

3

Almost Arrested

When we arrived at the railway station closest to the Piller home, we found it deserted. The last train had departed for the day. We stared down the track almost wistfully, a forlorn little group of five, gas masks dangling from our necks. We decided to go to the *Gare Centrale*, Antwerp's central station.

Everyone seemed to have converged on the *Gare Centrale*. The din of crying children and the desperate snarl of voices, shouts, and curses was deafening. Maurice shouldered his way into the train, the rest of us tightly behind. Every seat was taken, and the aisles were packed with people and baggage. We hunkered down on our valises and made the best of our discomfort.

When the train arrived in Brussels, the sun was setting; to our dismay, we discovered that there were no taxis available. We started walking towards Ukkle, the southern suburb of Brussels where Bronia and Marc lived. The long walk with valises was hard on my elderly in-laws, so our pace was slow. Again the streets were mostly deserted. The radio had been urging calm, so we assumed those people not fleeing were taking that advice.

As we walked, we saw Belgian soldiers, rifles in hand, knocking on doors and calling to the inhabitants of houses. They were polite, but determined.

—Come out! Come out! All German nationals must come out!

Doors cracked, windows opened.

—What have we done? I've lived here for five years!

—I'm sorry, *Madame*, *Monsieur*. You must come to the police station.

Because everyone had been required to register with the government, it was easy for the authorities to find the German nationals, and they were being rounded up as enemy aliens for deportation to the south of France.

The Germans gathered in tight, confused knots in the streets, some with suitcases, some with bundles, others with nothing, as if they expected that this was all a mistake.

Sullen-faced Belgian citizens watched from the sidewalk. A young woman pushed through a gathering crowd and spit on an old woman's shoe.

5. We hurried past jeering Belgians as German nationals were rounded up for deportation.

—Damn Nazi spy! Go home to your master!

Fright twisted the old woman's face. The sidewalk crowd surged forward. Soon they were jeering at the bewildered German nationals (most of whom were probably Jews who had fled Hitler).

Maurice and I and our group increased our pace away from the scene. None of us were Belgian citizens. Both our parents had come from Poland when we were small children. We were all considered citizens of that country. I looked at Maurice's face—he looked angry and worried, but only for a moment. He turned to me and smiled.

—It will be all right. You'll see.

I nodded, wanting to believe him.

We had stopped to rest on the doorstep of a private house just beyond the yellow light of a street lamp when a pair of burly policemen rounded the corner. They stopped and looked at us as if we each had two heads. Before we could say anything, they raised their rifles and screamed.

—Get up! Get up!

Instantly we bounded to our feet. Maurice raised his hands.

—For God's sake, don't shoot!

—Who are you? Don't move! Who are you?

—I'm just getting my identity card. See?

—Don't move! One move and I'll shoot!

By this time, we had all raised our hands. The hysterical policemen advanced tentatively, waving their rifles at each of us in turn. They would not let us show them our identification cards, which would have told them we were residents of Antwerp. Maurice tried to talk, but they silenced him. Still barking orders, they drove us toward an abandoned school building with the muzzles of their guns.

The building was crowded with refugees sitting and standing in the corridors and classrooms. Police stood guard, eyeing us nervously as we entered. We were taken to a large room and presented to an officer, a tall, mustachioed man whose calm demeanor had a positive effect on our captors.

The officer frowned at the policemen.

6. Suspected of being German parachutists, we were detained overnight in Brussels.

—Parachutists, huh? You think the Germans float down from the sky disguised as old men? Even they aren't that clever.

—I've heard they are dressed as priests and nuns! You can't trust anyone!

—Ask for their identification first, before you shoot, OK?

—How do we know they're not forgeries?

—Look at these people. Never mind, go on. Just don't shoot yourselves.

He turned to us.

—Your identification cards, please. I apologize. You can understand, though. We are all upset. Now then, you can leave if you wish, but I would urge you to stay for the night. My men are right, the Germans are parachuting in disguised as civilians. You are safer here.

Reluctantly, we stretched out on hard wooden benches that normally held students, rolled a bit of clothing beneath our heads, and endured a restless night amid the unceasing wail of air raid sirens.

* * *

Bronia was cooking when we arrived, her hands deep in dough. She was surprised to see us as we poured into the apartment, exhausted and hungry.

—Marc, make some coffee, please, and put out the bread and cheese.

Marc set about following his mother's orders. He was a good-looking boy with a shock of black hair and such a thin physique that had he not been tall, he would have seemed much younger than his fourteen years.

I sat down at the table where Bronia was kneading. White flour was dusted across her broad cheek.

—Bronia, we have to leave. If the Germans take over…. You know what they do to Jews.

—We should stay and fight the Nazis!

—Marc…!

Mr. Piller lowered himself into a chair and shook his head.

—No, Marc. Only dogs fight. The Nazis won't last.

Bronia looked at her father.

—Papa, I don't think I can leave. I promised the policeman responsible for this area. He said he would not arrest me if I stayed.

Bronia had married a German Jew and lived in Germany for a while before their marriage broke up and Bronia took Marc back to Belgium. Because of her marriage, she was considered a German national.

—It's not safe here, Bronia! What about the work you've been doing—against the Nazis? If Belgium is overrun….

Marc interrupted.

—She's burned everything. I saw her—in the boiler room downstairs.

—Thank you, Marc, but that doesn't change a thing. You have to leave, Bronia. You must.

But Bronia was stubborn. Or perhaps it would be better to say that she had a good heart. She had made a promise and she felt uncomfortable breaking it.

After two days—two days of listening to the ever more disheartening news of German incursions into Belgium and Holland—Bronia capitulated.

On May 13th, we found ourselves—seven of us now—in a crowded train fighting for space amid the chaos of frightened people. We had bought tickets to Courtrai, a Belgian town about an hour south, near the French border, and we had squeezed our way onto the train. Again, the train was packed with Belgian soldiers, this time heading to the French frontier. It was to be the last train out of Brussels that day.

The train jerked forward, and we steadied ourselves against each other. Marc had found a spot near a window, and he was staring out with the unbridled enthusiasm of a child who doesn't recognize danger. When we had gotten just beyond the city, he suddenly thrust an arm out the window.

—Look! An airplane!

7. Our spirits rose as we boarded a train bound for the French border.

The train ground to a halt, flinging us forward. A soldier, who had followed Marc's pointing finger, began to shout.

—Out! Out! It's a German bomber!

Hearts pounding, we bolted off the train. Maurice grabbed my hand and ran, dragging me away from the tracks. He turned and called back to his parents.

—Into the ditch! Into the ditch!

Maurice threw me to the ground.

4

Escape by Train

The German Messerschmidt screamed past. Its guns ripped into the earth along the track, splintering the wood and metal of the railway carriages. I pressed my hands against my ears and felt a scream rise in my throat.

And then it was all over. The air was still.

I raised my head slowly, fearful of what I might see. To my utter relief, I saw our train sitting unscathed in the bright sunlight of a spring afternoon on tracks that ran through farmland. Around me, heads poked above the tall ditch grass. A man in a train uniform shouted from the engine car.

—Get aboard! Come on! Everyone!

Wearily, the passengers approached the carriages. No one appeared hurt. I hugged Bronia, then helped my mother-in-law up the steps. Our hands were shaking so much we had trouble connecting. Back in the train, people found their places quietly, too unnerved to speak. Even Marc was subdued, perhaps out of deference to the feelings of others, for his face was alive with excitement. Oh, to be young and naïve!

The train moved forward, and I could almost hear the collective sigh of relief from the passengers. People began to talk quietly, to relax. Marc kept watch out the window. We had barely gotten underway when he jerked to attention.

—Here comes another one!

The train stopped, and we sprang out again. This time, I knew what to do. In a moment my face was buried in the sweet grass. I was grateful the weather had been unusually dry this month or I would have been eating mud.

The plane raked the train, then buzzed away. We were up again, more shaken than before. My knees felt like water. But what could we do? The train was filled with Belgian soldiers the Germans did not want to reach the French border.

The engine started. The train groaned forward. Marc yelled. And once again, we flung ourselves into the sunlight, into the grass. The attack ended as quickly as it had begun, and we scrambled up and back onto the train.

8. Nazi parachutists floated down like flowers around the train.

Then out again, then in. Then out, then in, throughout the night.

At dawn, we had traveled less than half the distance to Courtrai. We blinked at each other with hollow eyes. Our clothes were dirty and grass-stained. We licked dried lips and tried to ignore the growling in our stomachs. Even Marc was beginning to look worn.

Before the sun had risen far, we heard the whine of airplanes much higher than those that had been strafing us all night. I looked out the window and saw the sky blossom with dozens of strange, translucent flowers. They wafted lazily, and we watched, fascinated.

The train halted again, but this time a Belgian officer ordered us to stay inside. He jumped from the car, calling soldiers to follow him, and he led them away toward the descending flowers. Near the front of the train came the *rat-tat-tat!* of rifle fire.

They were parachutists, of course. A few drifted languidly toward the pasture near us.

—They're Belgians!

—What are they doing here? Attacking their own train?

The sudden thump of boots hitting the ground and a German curse banished the illusion. They were in disguise! Our soldiers were on them at once, screaming directives. A moment later, they marched four German soldiers past us.

—Why, they're children! Not much older than Marc!

—I'm not a child!

—I hope they caught them all.

—Children or not, they're Nazis. Shooting is too good for them!

I pulled my head in from the window and turned away, not wanting to see what happened to these Nazi teenagers. The Belgian officer climbed back into our car and sat down. When someone asked him about their uniforms, he explained that their mission had been to take over the train.

Any hope that the parachutists would somehow bring relief from the strafing quickly vanished when a few minutes after the train had lumbered forward, we heard the dreaded drone fol-

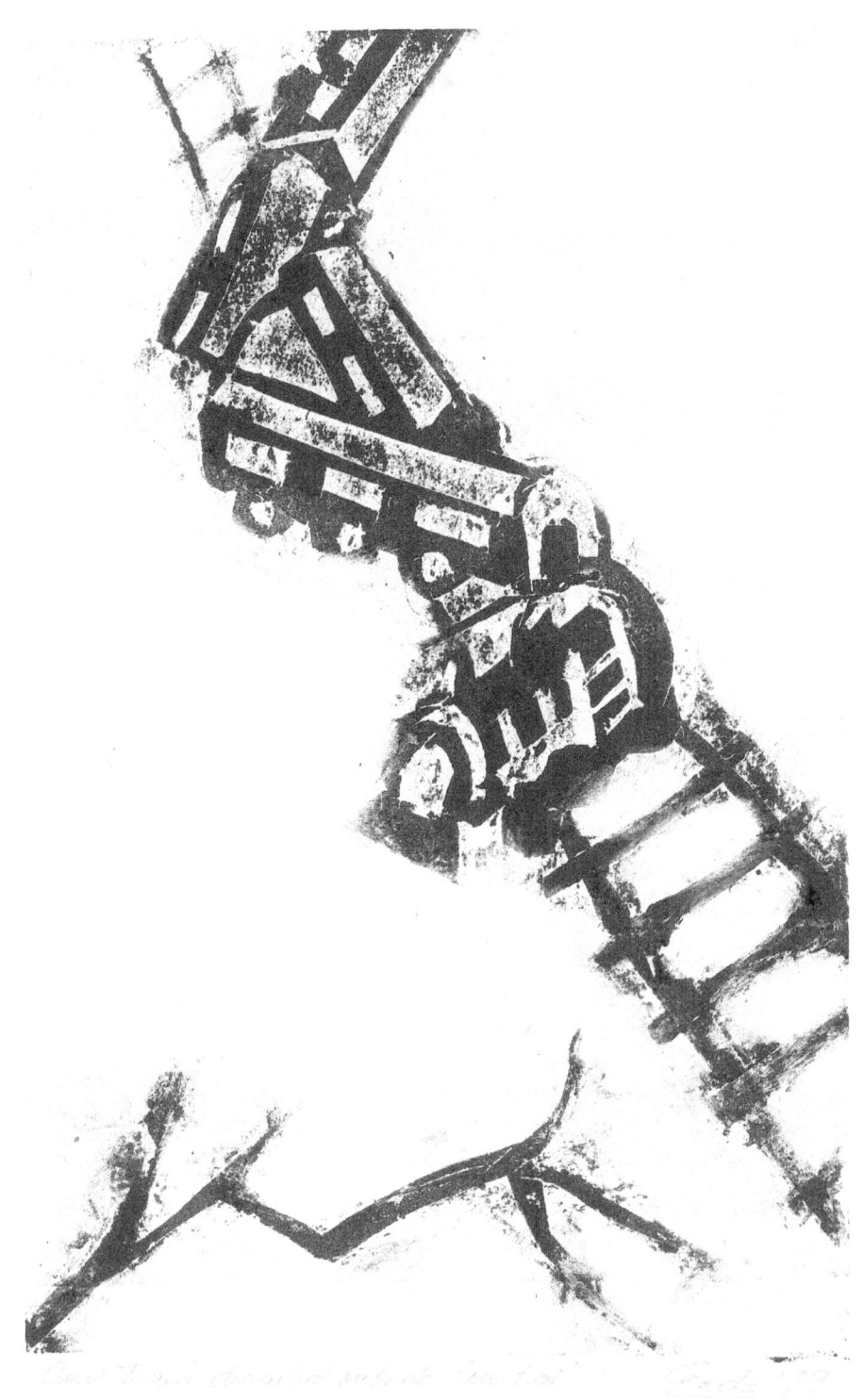

9. Before we reached Courtrai, the train jumped the tracks.

lowed by the squeal of the train's brakes. Once again, into the ditch we flew.

Forty-eight hours after we had left Brussels, we approached Courtrai, normally just an hour away. We were exhausted, filthy, thirsty, and famished. I didn't think it could get any worse. But as the night skyline began to fill with the dark shapes of blacked-out buildings, the train, as a final insult, jumped the rails. Like so many dice in a cup, we were tossed around inside the carriage until it came to rest halfway off the tracks.

Gingerly, we disentangled ourselves and stumbled out into the night, joining other ghostly figures drifting toward the station. Inside, we were greeted with the welcome sight of Red Cross workers. Cheerful women with red crosses on the breast pockets of their dresses handed us rolls and white cups topped with black coffee. I detested black coffee.

—Do you have cream?

—Sorry, dear.

I wrinkled my nose and drank it thirstily.

—Thank you, I can't remember when a cup of coffee tasted better. By the way, do you have any news about the war?

—Yes, haven't you heard? Holland has surrendered.

10. After 48 hours on the train, I was grateful for Red Cross coffee. (Original print shows red crosses.)

5
The Castle

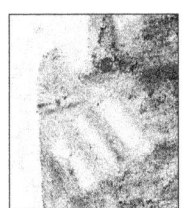

I lay on my back on the soft mattress and ran my hands across the smooth sheets. I'd almost forgotten what sheets felt like.

The mattress sagged as Maurice sat down on the edge. He began to take off his shoes.

—It has been an interesting three days, to say the least. I bet you never thought your honeymoon would be quite this exciting.

He leaned over and kissed me, just managing to stifle a yawn. It was well past midnight.

—Tomorrow should be much easier. It's just fourteen kilometers to Menin.

—And after that? Maybe we can see if there are boats from Calais, near Ostend.

We had the luxury of clean sheets and a soft bed by serendipity. After leaving the Red Cross at the train station, the seven of us wandered the streets looking for a place to stay. We had left our suitcases in the station, carrying only our coats. Every hotel we tried was full. And not just the rooms were occupied; the sofas and chairs in the lobbies were filled with sleeping refugees as well. Finally, we found ourselves near a small castle, a solid, square structure with narrow windows dotting somber stone walls. We were debating which way to turn when the thick wooden door to the castle swung open and a dark-haired woman stepped out, the amber light spilling from the interior.

—You look as if you could use a good meal and a bed.

She invited us in, seated us around a long dining table in a room of ancestral splendor, and served us a quick meal of fruit, cold meat, hardboiled eggs, potatoes, and beer. We ate ravenously and talked.

She lived alone in the castle. Her husband, a Belgian officer, had been called away to the French border, and her servants had gone home to their families. We asked her for news, and she told us that, indeed, the Dutch government had surrendered but that the Belgians were still fighting fiercely.

In the morning, we awoke refreshed and enjoyed a light breakfast with our hostess. We were eager to continue our journey, so

11. We found lodging in a small castle.

we bade her goodbye and walked toward the train station, our coats flung over our arms under the warming morning sun.

A dense cloud of smoke rolled up from the city ahead of us. We picked up our pace, winding our way among the streets toward the train station. My heart leapt to my throat as we rounded a corner onto a street that gave us a clear view of the station.

Ruin lay before us. Twisted girders and collapsed stone walls filled the space where the building had stood.

My mother-in-law stopped where she was and sat down on a doorstep. The rest of us ran forward. I looked for the woman who had given me coffee the night before, but I saw only a mass of unfamiliar people scrambling over the tumbled stone walls, calling, searching. My father-in-law found the place where we had left our luggage the night before. It was buried beneath tons of stone. Fortunately, we had our identity cards and money but nothing else save the clothes we were wearing and the coats over our arms.

Bronia broke away from our woeful group and found a railway employee. She returned with the news that a train had arrived from Menin, but it could not pass Courtrai because of the demolished rails; we might be able to take it back to Menin. We picked our way around the disheartening rubble, trying not to think of what—or who—might lie beneath and walked south along the railroad toward the border. After a short while we saw the train. We were allowed to board, and following a wait of several hours, we felt the train jerk forward. Our mood began to lift. We would soon be across the border, and we would be free.

As the train crawled through the Belgian countryside, farm buildings and grazing horses gave the impression of a land untouched by war. Only as the train came within sight of roads did we see stark evidence of a people on the move out of fear and hope. Long columns of refugees filled the roads. Cars, trucks, motorcycles, horse-drawn wagons, oxcarts, bicycles, baby perambulators, and, of course, tired feet transported the old and young and middle aged along the black roads. Children balanced on top of loads of belongings piled haphazardly or tied up in table

12. The train station was destroyed and all our luggage lost.

cloths or sheets. Now and then, trucks filled with soldiers forced the travelers off the road. They moved aside without complaint, and when the trucks had passed, the refugees climbed back onto the road, taking up their weary trek again.

We piled out of the train in Menin and walked south through the little town, passing the Menin Gate, a sober reminder of the war that was to end all wars. The white limestone arch bore the names of nearly 55,000 soldiers who perished in the First World War but whose remains were never found.

The street ended abruptly at a border crossing. Barbed wire stretched along either side of the red-and-white pole that barred the road and could be swung up to allow vehicles to cross. We dug into our pockets for our identification cards as we approached the small group of French soldiers smoking by the gate. An officer broke away from them.

—*Bonjour*. We're traveling to France from Antwerp. Here are our cards.

The officer threw down his cigarette and took the card. He glanced at it and handed it back.

—It doesn't matter. No one can go through.

—What do you mean?

—We have orders not to let anyone through.

We looked at each other in disbelief.

—You don't understand. We can't go back. We can't.

—I don't know anything, nothing. I have my orders. It's not just you, it's everyone. No one is allowed through.

—My God, we have traveled for days. We've been shot at, starved…! How can you do this to us?

—Go on back home. You cannot go through.

We yelled, we cried, we begged, but every word seemed only to stiffen the soldier's spine, to draw his mouth into a thinner, tighter line. Finally, he turned and paced back to his friends, who had been eyeing us tensely. The officer lit another cigarette.

—My God, Maurice, what are we going to do?

—I don't know. This isn't the only border crossing in France.

—He's right. We must try someplace else.

With a reluctance that turned our legs to lead, we forced ourselves to leave the border area. None of us talked of giving up, but the discouragement we felt was palpable. When the border was out of sight, we paused to discuss our next steps. To cross into France we would have to go west—the Germans threatened from the east. We were not sure how we would travel, whether by foot or train, but our course soon became obvious. We would find an open border with a friendlier patrol. Our only hope lay sixty kilometers away, in La Panne, just north of Dunkirk.

What Ida, Maurice, and the others could not have known when they tried to cross the border at Menin was that the German Blitzkrieg had also struck northern France. Whether he knew this or was merely following orders, the officer could not have let them through without allowing them to fall into the hands of the Germans.

As they traveled west toward the coast and hoped-for freedom, Ida and her family discovered that the British Expeditionary Force was running away, too, and the French and Belgian armies were struggling to survive. When the British tanks and trucks had first rumbled through the Belgian towns, the citizens had poured into the streets, tossing flowers at them and waving black, yellow, and red Belgian flags. But the German attack squeezed the British, French, and Belgian armies tighter and tighter. Soon Belgium's citizens met the fleeing British with jeers and ridicule. By May 21, the Germans had surrounded some of the British Expeditionary Force and remnants of other Allied armies—about 400,000 men in all—in Dunkirk (France) and along the coast to La Panne (Belgium). The soldiers—along with thousands of innocent refugees—had their backs to the sea.

13. Barbed wire and determined guards stopped us at the French border.

6

Toward La Panne, near Dunkirk

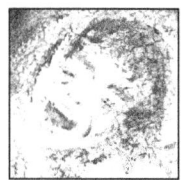

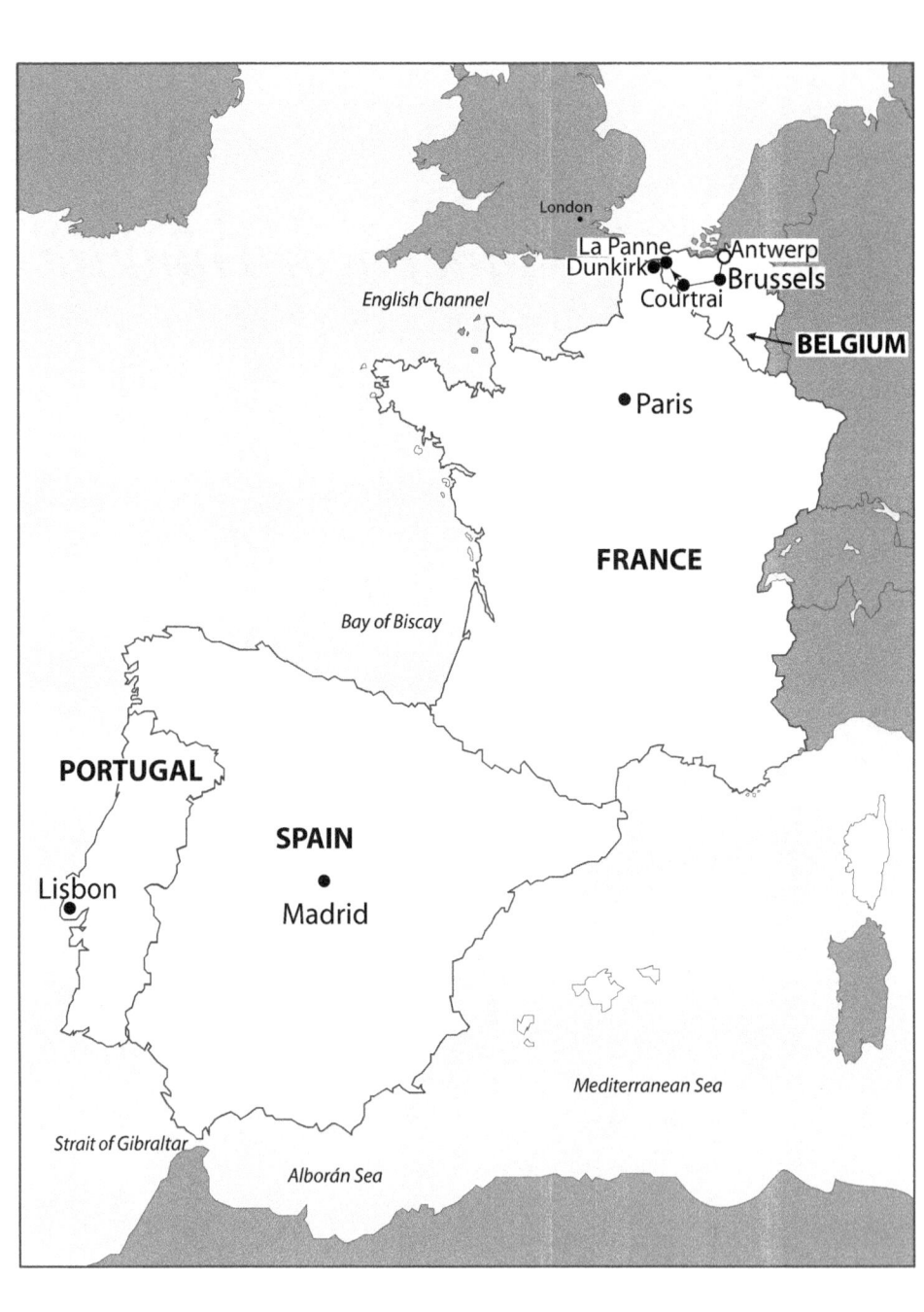

Now it was our turn to join the flow of refugees plodding along the roads of Belgium. It was our turn to find our way across a landscape that looked more and more like a war zone. Tanks had churned the farmland to mud. Bombs had gouged craters in the earth. Abandoned cars had been crushed and burned. The ground was littered with shattered glass and shreds of paper.

We spent our days trudging on foot, calling for rides to passing trucks or buses, finding a car or horse cart to carry Maurice's parents a little way ahead. Nights found us huddled together in ditches or behind farm buildings, struggling to sleep amid the disembodied cries of other hidden refugees and the *thud-thud!* and *tat-tat-tat!* of the *Luftwaffe*. The waning moon cast its glow into the dark crevasses where we hid, too exhausted and frightened to do more than snatch at sleep.

We became intimately acquainted with the angle and depth of ditches, the sharp edges of grass trampled into the mud by the many refugees before us. Now ours were the haunted faces stared at by passengers in fleeing cars. Now we were part of the angry, silent crowds who stumbled aside for the stone-faced British and Belgian soldiers who careened by in crowded trucks as they retreated from the advancing Germans.

There was an immediacy to our lives that left little room for fear of the future or memories of the past. We lived in the moment, and each moment held a lifetime of emotions—fear, shock, surprise, anguish.

We saw a woman kneeling in the churned mud alongside the road, her mouth a black hole in a stark white face. In her arms lay the riddled body of a child. Blood soaked the ground in a widening pool, her desperate plea of *Help my baby!* unanswerable.

The sun was setting over the English Channel when we arrived at La Panne, three miles from Dunkirk in France. Soldiers and civilians filled the streets. The stench of burning oil filled the air.

On our first night, we found a basement to sleep in, and we lay on the cold stone floor using our coats for blankets. In the morning,

14. German planes strafed fleeing refugees on the road to the coast.

15. A woman wailed for help for her dead child.

we rose stiffly and made our way out into the watery sunlight to look for breakfast. We walked down to the long flat beach that swept toward the sea. It was littered with abandoned, smoking vehicles. Soldiers in khaki uniforms hunkered in bomb craters and hastily dug foxholes, grim-faced. There were few places for them to hide as they waited for boats and dinghies and ships to whisk them to safety in Britain, a place that, it soon became apparent, was open only to them.

The local farmers had quickly run out of fruits and vegetables in the press of hungry refugees and soldiers, who didn't wait for the farmers but tore vegetables from the fields. The farmers offered piles of white and brown eggs, boiled to preserve them because there was no refrigeration. (We bought them eagerly at first, but as the days passed and the war progressed, we soon tired of a diet of hardboiled eggs.)

That night we found rooms on the second floor of a house. Grateful to have beds again, we fell into them exhausted. Unknown to us, Hitler had halted his attack, fearful that his generals had over-reached their strength. There was a two-day pause in the fighting before the German military might was unleashed again. The *Luftwaffe* returned to La Panne, fire-bombing it during the day so that the flames would light the sky and illuminate the fleeing English soldiers at night.

We were forced back into the basement, where we cowered with eleven other people, including a baby. At first Marc refused to join us, saying he wanted to sleep in a bed. Bronia insisted, however, so he spent a fitful night with us, listening to the whine and scream of airplanes and the answering fire of anti-aircraft guns. Bronia sang to keep everyone's spirits up.

The next day, we staggered out into the devastated town. The house above us had been mostly destroyed. Very little was left except a staircase and parts of the floors and walls. A man stumbled down the shattered stairs looking dazed as we emerged from the basement. Bronia dragged Marc up the stairs and showed him the bed he had given up. It was riddled with bullets.

16. We found shelter in a basement in La Panne, near Dunkirk.

Exhausted from the lack of sleep, we found our way to the boardwalk that ran along the beach and bought enough eggs to satisfy our hunger. There was no coffee to be had anywhere. Again we looked at the beach. Many more vehicles had been hit; black clouds billowed into the morning sky. Dotting the sand now were the prostrate bodies of young English soldiers, their arms flung out, rifles beyond their reach.

The sea was littered with bodies, blood, and debris. English boats swarmed toward the shore, plucking up surviving British soldiers and what appeared to be a few soldiers from other Allied armies. They left us to watch in despair as the boats motored or rowed out to larger ships, which could not come near the shore because of the shallowness of the water and the continued strafing by German planes. Civilians, too, tried to leave in whatever would float long enough to make the crossing.

Disheartened, we returned to the basement where once again we heard the distant drone of German planes. Where was the Royal Air Force, we wondered. Why was this stretch of Belgium being abandoned? By now we knew that Antwerp had fallen, and so had Brussels. Was all hope for our country—and for us—now gone?

Unbeknownst to us, there was an unexploded bomb lodged in one of the basement windows. Luckily, it did not explode while we were there. That night, again, the *Luftwaffe* returned to La Panne.

In the morning, we awoke, exhausted but with the realization that we had, in fact, finally been able to sleep. As we stretched and roused ourselves, we noticed a strange absence of sound outside. The rumbling sounds of war, the clatter of refugees moving along the streets, the cries of the farmers selling their boiled eggs—all were gone. Suddenly, the quiet was broken by a high, youthful voice. He was too far away for us to understand what language he was speaking.

Maurice and I scrambled out of the ruined stairway into the empty street. The others followed quickly. Around us, the town

17. Every kind of vessel was put to use by people desperate to cross the English Channel.

18. A hellish light from incendiary bombs lit the town at night.

19. The beach was littered with the bodies of dead English soldiers.

20. German soldiers biked into La Panne to tell us we were "saved."

lay in shambles, like a child's sand castle kicked by a cruel foot, yet the blue sky, the high clouds, and the melodious song of a blackbird perched atop the remains of a chimney gave a surreal air to the scene. I turned to look down the street and caught Maurice's arm to get his attention.

Close by, two soldiers in sharp, field-gray uniforms straddled their bicycles and chatted with a woman carrying a basket of eggs. They must be Dutch, I thought; Belgians, Americans, and English soldiers all wore khaki-colored uniforms.

One of them touched his helmet as if he were tipping his hat to the women, and he smiled. The two soldiers then rode past her, and as they did, one of them called out in the same youthful voice we had heard before.

—*Wir sind da. Ihr seid gerettet!*

My God! Germans!

Pushing their bikes, they strolled toward us, repeating their news cheerfully.

—We are here. You are saved!

We stood, our breath snatched from our throats, as they approached.

—*Guten Morgen!*

We could not find our voices. Though German was one of the languages we spoke, we were afraid to acknowledge it. The young soldiers—no older than I!—were unperturbed.

—Are you from La Panne? No? Well, then, you can go home now. We are here! Belgium has joined the Fatherland! You are safe!

The escape of the British Expeditionary Force (BEF) (which comprised almost all of England's experienced soldiers and officers) along with part of the French army from the beaches around Dunkirk and La Panne across the English Channel was one of the great feats and great disasters of the war. Of the 250,000-man British force trapped in northern Europe, some 215,000 were whisked away on every conceivable seaworthy vessel. The rescue was so successful—beyond the British government's wildest calculation— in part because Hitler, for complex reasons, halted his attack on Dunkirk from May 24 to May 26, allowing more soldiers to escape.

Unfortunately for the forces confronting Germany in Continental Europe, almost all of Britain's experienced troops were either dead or back in England. France begged Britain to send its Royal Air Force (RAF) fighters against the Germans, but the British refused. Nearly all of the BEF's heavy equipment—trucks, tanks, armaments—had been abandoned on the Continent, and Britain was fearful of leaving their island nation unguarded. The French would bitterly claim that the British were willing to fight "to the last Frenchman," but with their own ineptitude, petty politics, and poor planning, France's leaders and generals also contributed to their nation's defeat.

7
Return to Antwerp

One by one, the countries along the German front were falling. On May 11, Luxembourg had lasted one day under the German assault. The Netherlands fell on May 15. And now, on May 28, Belgium had been crushed beneath the boot of Germany. It was obvious the English would be of no help, and who knew how long the French army, vast as it was, would last. For two days, Maurice, his family and I vacillated—what should we do?

—The English will come back!

—Those cowards!

—Then the Americans will come. They won't abandon Europe.

—How can we know? They are so far away, and they have shown no interest in our squabbles.

Indeed, the United States government under Franklin Roosevelt watched the machinations in Europe with a nervous eye but with no inclination to join in. We all knew about the SS *St. Louis*. In 1939, the United States had failed to take in this shipload of German Jewish refugees seeking asylum when they were turned away from their destination, Cuba. Roosevelt's government had allowed them to be forced back to Europe.

Our options, then, were to try to get through into France or to return home. But we soon heard that the French border was closed on this western edge, too. The French were fighting for their lives. Finally, we saw that our only choice was to return to Antwerp.

So that morning we stumbled out of the basement, rolled our coats beneath our arms, and turned our disheartened faces toward home. We did not wail or weep. So far, we had survived what the Germans had thrown at us; perhaps our luck would hold. And if it didn't? We felt we had no other choice.

Other men, women, and children were already on the road as we walked out of La Panne. The beaches were empty now, except for the destroyed and abandoned vehicles and the limp bodies of dead soldiers that shifted with the tide.

In their haste, the British had abandoned their trucks and other vehicles. Maurice walked up to one and opened the door.

—What are you doing, Maurice?

—Looking for keys.

He slammed the door and rejoined us.

—There is no reason to walk if we can ride.

Of course! My clever husband! He was the only one among us who could drive. In Antwerp, his shop had sold and repaired radios. Before his business had started to slow in the bad economy, Maurice had owned a car that he used to deliver radios his repairman had fixed.

When we passed another truck, he peeked in the window.

—Keys! Come on!

He swung up into the truck's cab. I helped his mother and father squeeze in beside him and then joined Bronia, Cylia, and Marc in the back beneath a canvas stretched across ribs of metal. Our spirits lifted. We smiled at each other, feeling the satisfaction that comes from thinking you have outwitted fate—at least to a small degree.

Through the broken window in the back of the truck, I heard Maurice mutter that he hoped the truck had gas, and then watched him turn over the engine. There was a hesitant grinding sound, then a roar as it sprang to life.

—We're off!

But oh, how cruel fate can be! I had not seen a British plane in all the time we were in La Panne. Not one pilot to look down on us and take pity, not one to fight back against the Germans. As we pulled out into the road, inching our way through the tide of humanity, I looked backward at the smoldering ruins of the town and saw the small speck, an insect-sized speck, of fuselage and wings buzzing toward us. Marc recognized it first.

—It's British!

Outside the truck, around us, stricken faces turned skyward, then everyone began to run toward the fields, diving under the few trees, cowering in craters left by German bombs. The truck jerked to a halt, its doors flew open. We scrambled out.

Tat-tat-tat-tat-tat!

Bullets tore down the length of the canvas top and through the cab. A moment later, the plane had vanished into the still sky.

21. Turned away at the French border, we made our way back to Antwerp.

—Idiot!
—What's the matter with him!
—He thinks we're Germans!

Of course he did, even though we were driving a British truck. By now all the British had fled or been killed. So who was left to drive their vehicles but the Germans?

Shakily, I looked at the others. No one was harmed, but every face was pale. Maurice set his mouth and stalked back to the truck. The rest of us climbed in. Maurice cranked the engine. Our pounding hearts began to slow and we sat back. I closed my eyes. And heard the buzz.

Someone cried out. Maurice jerked the wheel and headed us toward the ditch as the British fighter roared low overhead. Puffs of dust exploded on the road where we had been moments before.

As soon as it passed, Maurice tried again. The road was clear of walking refugees. Obviously, we were too dangerous to be near. None of us sat back and relaxed this time. Our ears and eyes stayed alert, waiting.

And when it came again, we bounded off the road with so much bouncing that it was impossible to hold on. Finally, the truck came to a stop. We fled again. But this time, when we had picked ourselves up from the muddy ditch, we hung back, reluctant to approach the truck. We had gone no more than two kilometers.

—Come on. We'd better get away from this thing before he comes back.

And so we continued, walking when we had to, catching rides when we could. At the city of Ghent, half way to Antwerp, we negotiated with a man who had an ox and cart to carry Maurice's parents. They clambered onto the uncomfortable wooden cart and bounced along as we followed wearily behind.

When we arrived at the Schelde River, a broad waterway that runs along the edge of Antwerp and made it the biggest port on the European continent, we discovered that the Belgians had flooded the tunnel beneath it during the German invasion. The German army had quickly assembled a shaky bridge of row boats and wooden planks, but the oxcart driver announced he could not take his cart across such an unstable structure. Maurice's parents climbed off. We paid the man and picked our way across the bridge under the watchful eyes of German guards.

Maurice and I accompanied the elder Mr. and Mrs. Piller, Bronia, Marc, and Cylia to the Piller home, and then took a tram to my parents' house. I was eager to see them again after such a long absence. Surely, like us, they would be home again.

We entered Omegangstraat to find the street quiet. No bombs had fallen. The shop where my father had spent so many hours and the apartment above it where we lived stood unscathed. I took out my house key, which I had managed to hang onto through all our trials, and fit it into the lock. It would not turn.

—What's the matter with it?

—Maybe it's jammed. I don't understand. Let's try the back door.

We knocked on the door of the next-door neighbors' house and were let into their backyard. A wall separated our two gardens. Looking into ours, I could see nothing amiss. The shed where Papa stored extra merchandise, the outhouse we never used, the back door to the house—all seemed perfectly normal.

Maurice boosted me over the wall, then followed. I ran to the back door, found that the key worked, and flung the door open, calling for my parents and my sister Rosa. I assumed my older sister Annie and her husband and son would be at their apartment nearby.

The downstairs rooms consisted of a large store and a small office. I stopped and gaped when I entered the store. Nearly everything was gone. The long shelves that had held bolts of fabric were now empty. Only Papa's big desk remained.

I looked at Maurice, who looked as confused as I felt. With considerable trepidation, we climbed the steps to the apartment.

It was a two-story apartment with a living room, a kitchen, and my parents' bedroom on the first floor, and a bedroom where my sister Rosa and I slept on the second. There was a landing between the two floors, and off this landing was the toilet. There was no bathroom in the house—that is, no room with a bath or shower. We normally bathed once a week at a nearby bathhouse, and because I was on a swim team, I showered after swimming. When my sister Annie married and moved into an apartment with a bathroom, I thought it was a luxury to soak in her tub. Throughout our travels, we had not had a chance to bathe. I had taken to wearing a headscarf to cover my dirty hair.

Now we stepped into the living room. Chairs, tables, cupboards—every piece of furniture but the heaviest was gone, and along with them all the rugs, linens, dishes, decorations, photographs on the walls, even my wedding presents. Then I saw the large, heavy trunk. I dropped to the floor beside the trunk and threw back the lid. Empty!

The wedding dress was gone!

It had been borrowed from a friend. I had intended to return it when I got back from my honeymoon.

Maurice reached out a hand and helped me to my feet. I called again for my parents, a hand over my heart as if I could stop it from climbing up my throat. Maurice and I ran up to the top floor.

A single, large bed remained, along with a dresser, which someone had tried to move but had not gotten far with. The bed had been stripped, and the dresser drawers gaped open, their contents gone. One of the few things that remained was a small, leather photograph album of mine with pictures of my family and friends.

Shaken, we made our way back down the stairs and on down to the shop. Maurice unlocked the shop's front door—at least the lock wasn't broken!—and we stepped out into the street. I looked back at the house, angry and confused.

Across the street, a door opened. An elderly woman, leaning on a cane, hobbled across to us.

—I didn't expect to see you back! I thought you had moved.

—No, no, we've been trying to get into France. Do you know where my parents and sister are?

—No. When the trucks came, I thought they had come for your things.

22. My parents were gone, and their store and home had been ransacked.

—What trucks?

—Why, there were two Red Cross trucks. The drivers and a couple of men moved everything out and drove away. I assumed they needed material for the hospital.

I groaned and sagged against the wall. Not for a moment did I think my parents had moved. Where would they go with all those household goods? No, somehow we had been burglarized. It was hard to believe the Red Cross would have been involved in something so criminal but a driver and a few of his corrupt friends might have.

We thanked the woman and turned back into the building. Maurice carefully locked the door behind us and I led the way upstairs. Exhausted and disheartened, we threw ourselves down on the bare mattress of the one remaining bed, wondering what fresh insults awaited us.

8
Surviving under the Nazis

A few days later, Maurice and I sat at the dining room table in my parents' living room, counting the few bills and coins we had left.

—We're going to have to do something. It's no use pretending people are interested in getting their radios repaired with money so tight.

I looked around the almost-empty room. We had borrowed the chairs we were sitting on, but there was little else—certainly nothing we could sell.

—We're strong. We can find work, surely.

Fear and uncertainty pervaded the Jewish quarter in Antwerp. It had been a prosperous center of the diamond trade; everyone either had worked in diamonds or was related to someone who had. Maurice's father and sister Cylia both worked in the business. Even I had worked at the tedious task of sorting tiny diamonds for a while. Cylia had found me the job when I had quit working at my father's store where I had sold dry goods and kept the books. I had quit because my mother and father had not approved of my wanting to marry Maurice. They wanted me to become a doctor and to marry a man with better prospects than those of the owner of a radio repair shop. They were afraid I would live a Bohemian life. But my passion lay in art, and my heart belonged to Maurice. Twice Maurice had asked for my hand in marriage, and twice he was refused. I could not marry without their permission until I turned twenty-one. Fortunately, a few months before my twenty-first birthday, Bronia took the train from Brussels and held a private conversation with my parents. Whatever she said changed their minds, and they opened their hearts to Maurice and helped us plan our wedding.

My feelings about my wedding day were mixed now. It had been the happiest day of my life, but life after it had become one long nightmare, and we were not sure when or how the nightmare would end.

Neither of us had any doubt about the fate of the Jews under the Germans. It was true that they had not singled out Jews in

Belgium for special treatment. We were not yet required to wear the yellow Star of David on our coats, and we were under the same curfew as everyone else—seven at night to seven in the morning. Yet we knew too well their history with the Jews in Germany and Poland. My mother's sister and her two little sons had fled Poland and had stayed with us for a while the year before, after Hitler had invaded Poland. Her stories sent chills down our spines. And *Kristallnacht*, the night when German citizens destroyed the homes and business of their Jewish neighbors, had occurred less than a year before. Everyone we knew had a friend or relative who had escaped the Nazis. Antwerp had swelled with refugees. Alongside the worries over money and the future, the uncertainty about what had happened to my parents and sisters gnawed at me.

Many people had fled Antwerp and were now straggling back, defeated in their attempts to escape or too short of money to continue. I questioned them anxiously about my family, but there was never any news.

One day we saw a line of young men waiting to board buses. When we asked where they were going, they said they had signed up for jobs in Germany. Unemployment was high; there was no other work.

We were horrified and tried to talk them out of their decision, but they shrugged us off. They must work or starve, they told us. We were not certain then what fate awaited them, but we knew it would be worse than their life in Antwerp.

As Maurice and I walked away, thinking about the strangely serene occupation by Germany, whose leader was so openly anti-Semitic, a truck rumbled by laden with furniture held in place with ropes. The familiar faces of a neighbor family peered palely out the window. We knew they had tried to escape. Now they were returning home defeated. It was a scene we witnessed often.

—That's it!

—What?

—I know someone with a truck and a German driver's license. We'll hire him to help us move refugees back home. Think how

23. Unemployed Belgians signed up for work in Germany.

24. German troops sang as they marched through the streets.

eagerly we would have paid to have someone come pick us up from La Panne or even Ghent.

—Why, that's a great idea!

The man with the truck was amenable to the idea, and the three of us headed south to look for tired refugees, some of whom had fled with household goods only to have their cars or trucks break down. They were relieved to have help in returning to Antwerp. In some cases, refugees who returned on foot hired us to retrieve the goods that they had been forced to leave behind.

One night we brought home a family of seven. By the time we had entered Antwerp, the curfew was only minutes away. Fearing arrest, we took them to our apartment for the night. As soon as we had locked the door, we heard the nightly clap of boots on the road outside and the rhythmic chant of German soldiers singing as they marched by.

For the next few weeks, we hauled Jewish refugees back to Antwerp. We also spent hours listening to the radio or visiting Maurice's family. We grew restless with the occupation, the growing scarcity of food, the ever-present German uniforms.

One day, while Maurice was visiting friends, I stepped out to buy some food. My basket was heavy as I fitted the key into the new lock on the door of the closed and shuttered shop. As I entered, I heard someone walk across the floor upstairs. I called Maurice's name, but fear kept my voice low.

I approached the stairs cautiously and began to ascend. I heard a determined walk, the scrape of a chair. Whoever it was had sat down at the table. I paused for a moment, wondering what to do, then took the stairs quickly. As I rose to the top and the room came into view, my heart skipped a beat.

Mama! My beautiful, black-haired Mama looked up with weary eyes from a face pinched with exhaustion. She rose as I dropped the basket, and we fell into each other's arms.

9

Advice and Dissent

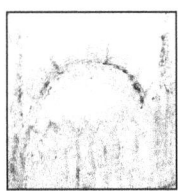

My mother Marinya's wide face and blue eyes held the terror and uncertainty of the journey she, my father Samuel, Rosa, Annie, Max, and Charly had endured since the night of my wedding.

Upon word of the invasion, they had packed valises and fled with many other Jewish citizens of Antwerp. Thinking Maurice and I were in Ostend, they initially traveled by train to that seaside town. When they could not find us, they continued to flee in front of the German advance, finally making their way to the outskirts of Paris where they were trapped between the frightened citizens of the city and the Nazi war machine. My father had been hopeful that the French and English would push the German army back.

When the Germans marched into Paris on June 14, my family was able to get into the city where they were helped by the Red Cross. The life of a refugee—six people to a small room awaiting an uncertain future—was too much for my mother. She and my father were in their fifties. She had trekked wearily home to see what life was like in Antwerp under the Germans.

My parents had lived in Antwerp since I was two years old. Originally from Poland, they had spent many years in Vienna, where my father had been the head decorator for the Viennese court and where they had lived a life of culture and luxury. When the Austro-Hungarian Empire collapsed, they were forced to return to Krakow, Poland, because in Vienna they had become "stateless." But anti-Semitism, bad weather, and lifestyle had inspired them to move once again. This time, they relocated to Antwerp where my mother's sister and some other family members lived. They established a store selling supplies to the decorating trade. My father labored all day and into the night to make a meager living in those Depression years, with my mother helping—a rarity for a married woman—as well as taking care of the house and their three daughters, and keeping kosher, for they were religious. The sight of the shelves stripped bare sank my mother's heart.

In the meantime, Maurice and I began to talk of leaving. We had no children, we were young enough, and we were growing increasingly uneasy with the German presence. While we were debating our departure, my sister Annie returned unexpectedly. She had left Max and their three-year-old son Charly in Paris with my father and Rosa. Like my mother, she had come back to Antwerp to see what life was like under the Germans. We discussed our plans with Annie, and we agreed that she and Max and Charly would run away with us. She left a few days later to return to Paris and wait for us there.

When we told Mama and Maurice's parents that we were going to leave Belgium in search of freedom, they were violently opposed to the idea.

—You can't! It's too dangerous!
—Where will you go?
—How do you expect to pay for all this?
—We have about $80 in francs. We'll go south, to Spain or Africa.
—Spain! That dictator Franco will throw you right back.
—We'll get visas. We'll go to the United States.
—Ha! The American's don't want Jews!
—It is better to stay here. The Germans won't last forever.

But Maurice and I had discussed our options and opportunities at length. We needed to take this chance to make a life for ourselves somewhere where we would not be constantly looking over our shoulders.

On August 5th, we packed a small bag (made of leftover upholstery material so it did not look like a suitcase) with a minimum of clothing and my precious photo album, which now included a few photos from our wedding. I tucked our $80-worth of franc notes into a small pouch and pinned it inside my bra. We were ready to leave. Though we were leaving in hope of finding a better life, there was only sadness at our parting. Mama and I held each other tightly. When would we see each other again?

Eighty dollars was a reasonable amount of money in those days, but we did not know how long we would need to make it last, so we began our journey hitchhiking. Our first ride took us along a road leading south, out of the city. The buildings became

25. I hugged my mother goodbye, wondering if I would ever see her again.

more scattered and barns and farm houses set in wide, flat fields came to dominate the landscape. Refugees rattled by in the other direction, traveling in trucks and cars or pushing prams or carts. They looked past us to the city, some hollow-eyed and anxious, others obviously relieved. We hoped for the best for them but hurried on our own journey. We had no idea whether we were right to leave Antwerp, but we felt we were traveling in the right direction, toward freedom.

A few kilometers beyond the city, we were let out. We found ourselves walking beside the road, our feet swishing through damp grass, our fingers intertwined. Our enjoyment of each other and the countryside was interrupted by the sound of a truck behind us, the grinding of gears, the smell of motor oil. It was gaining on us, so we stepped farther from the shoulder and glanced back to see if we were far enough. I clutched Maurice's hand tighter. It was a German truck with a canvas-covered back similar to the British truck in which we had tried to escape from La Panne. Surreptitiously, I touched the place where the money was pinned, then glanced at the carpet bag Maurice gripped. Did it look suspicious? What would they say to two citizens traveling south when everyone else was traveling north? But maybe they would just drive by. Why should they bother with us?

The truck's breaks squealed as it stopped beside us. The driver, a cigarette pinched between the fingers of one hand, leaned out the window. Sweat dripped down his nose.

—*Morgen! Ist heiss, nicht? Wo wollt Ihr hin?*—Morning! It's hot, isn't it? Where are you headed?

Maurice and I dared not look at each other. We had to think independently and fast. The smiling German waited.

Maurice sputtered an answer in awkward German, mispronouncing the words and mangling the grammar, though we both spoke the language fluently.

—Just fifty kilometers. We're looking for my wife's parents. They're trying to get back to Antwerp, and we're going to help them.

The German spoke to the thin, young soldier beside him.

26. While hitchhiking, we were picked up by German military trucks.

—Shall we take them?

—Sure, why not?

The driver turned back to us, where we stood riveted to the road, and spoke loudly and slowly, as if we were children.

—We are going fifty kilometers. We will help you. Get in the back of the truck.

He broadly gestured his cigarette-clutching hand toward the rear of the vehicle.

—Come, come! It's a free ride. Climb into the back.

Maurice, who seemed to have vast resources of optimism, tugged my hand.

So with some misgivings, we walked to the back of the truck where we found, to our dismay, a half dozen soldiers leaning on their rifles and sitting on long benches that ran the length of both sides of the truck bed. One of them reached out a hand to me. I did not want to touch this German's hand, but I took it anyway and allowed him to pull me up into the truck. Maurice clambered up behind me and we huddled together where the soldiers had made a place for us.

They were friendly enough and tried to strike up a conversation, but we feigned ignorance of their language, and gradually their efforts died away. After that we rode in silence, all the while wondering if the driver would allow us to leave. Our relief was enormous when we felt the truck grind to a halt more than an hour after we had started. We exchanged glances, forced a smile toward our fellow passengers, and scrambled out of the truck bed. All we could see of the driver was his hand waving out the window as he proceeded on down the road.

—That wasn't so bad!

—Do you think we can do it again?

Indeed we could and we did. We took up our hike along the road, and when we heard the grind of gears behind us, Maurice put out his hand to flag them down.

This driver was as accommodating as the last one had been. Again, we told him that we were going to meet our parents just fifty kilometers down the road so that we could bring them back to Antwerp.

This time the driver was alone, and he gestured for us to squeeze into the truck beside him. It gave me no pleasure to sit so close to a German soldier, but Maurice acted relaxed and friendly, nodding and smiling at everything the soldier said while at the same time implying that he could not understand a word of it.

We bounced along the road for nearly half an hour when suddenly the driver veered onto a dirt road to the left. Maurice, who had his arm around the back of my seat, squeezed my shoulder. The smile died on his face as he looked out the window. I followed his gaze and took in a sharp breath.

Ahead of us, at the end of the narrow, rutted road were the long strands of barbed wire, guarded gate, and makeshift tents of a hastily assembled military camp. Beyond the wire, German soldiers marched in formation past shiny tanks. The driver tooted the truck's horn, and the guards by the gate jumped to action, throwing the gate wide and waving toward the truck. The driver shifted, stepped on the gas, and drove us past the barbed wire and into the German army camp.

10

Unpleasant Surprises in Paris

The driver halted the truck just inside the gate, climbed down without giving us a second glance, and disappeared around the side of the vehicle. Maurice reached across me and squinted into the side-view mirror. I felt the back of the truck sag and jump a little, as if someone had climbed up into it, then climbed down. A moment later, the driver walked by carrying a wooden box. As he passed, Maurice sat up quickly.

We watched the driver carry the box to one of the tents, stopping to talk to a man lounging outside. He then disappeared behind the tent flap. We had time to look around, but other soldiers walked around the truck without giving it a glance. I hardly knew what to think. I had little time to speculate, because shortly the driver reappeared, walked to the truck, and climbed back behind the wheel. He smiled at us, started the engine, and spoke again.

—Sorry I had to stop. I'm delivering film.

Delivering film? Was that all? I sagged against the seat, feeling lightheaded with relief. When the driver put his hands up as if he were holding a camera and pressed an imaginary shutter button, I nodded with more enthusiasm than was necessary to show I understood.

As the truck turned around and headed back out of the gate, I felt Maurice relax beside me. We exchanged glances and small smiles. So far our journey was going surprisingly well. When we came to the French border, we found the border had, for all practical purposes, disappeared. Now that the countryside was under the control of the Germans, we did not need papers to pass from Belgium into France. If only our good fortune would continue....

When we reached the outskirts of Paris, however, we were met with the stiff-armed *Heil Hitler!* of a guard and long strings of barbed wire twisted into a barrier on either side of the road.

We thanked the driver as he deposited us at the checkpoint. The guard watched us without moving, looking implacable. A German officer sauntered out of a building as we approached the guard. We mixed our German with good French as we explained that my family was staying with the Red Cross in Neuilly, a Paris

27. Paris had fallen and refugees were being turned away. How would we get through?

suburb. After some hesitation, the officer not only passed us through but decided to accompany us to ensure our safety, though I wondered whether it was also to ensure that we were telling the truth.

Whatever his motives, he drove us to the Red Cross offices. We expected to find Annie, Max, and Charly waiting for us, though Papa and Rosa might not be there; we knew they planned to return to Antwerp. But everyone had left the day before. We were heartbroken and wondered what could have prevented my sister Annie and her family from waiting for us as she had said they would.

The Paris streets were filled with German soldiers and their vehicles. They treated Paris as if it were theirs, sipping wine in outdoor cafes, touring museums, wandering through elegant gardens. The Parisians eyed them with fear and disdain.

Yet this was Paris, the City of Lights. I had never been to Paris.

—Let's stay!

—In Paris?

—For just a little while, just to see the Eiffel Tower, Notre Dame.

So we did. For three days we toured the city. Our time there was the honeymoon I had not had, though a strange one in which we spent as little money as we could and slept for free in a room provided by the Red Cross with no bathroom and only a toilet down the hall.

Eventually, we began to hear rumors from other Jews we had met at the shelter.

—Have you heard about Gurs?

—What is it?

—It was a prison camp for Spaniards fleeing Franco.

—So?

—They are rounding up Jews, German Jews now, but who knows who will be next. It is terrible there, I hear, just terrible.

Not enough food, we heard; not enough medicine. People were dying. Shaken, Maurice and I decided it was time to leave Paris

28. The Germans were everywhere, but Maurice and I lingered to see the sights.

behind. We would have to make our way through the rest of occupied France and then through Vichy France before we could think of finding freedom. The honeymoon was over.

With the German advance, the French government fled to Bordeaux, and hundreds of Parisians poured into the roads heading south. The Germans entered Paris on June 14, and on June 21 the French government formally surrendered at Rethondes—the same city and railway carriage in which the Germans had surrendered at the end of the World War I.

France was now divided in two. The northern three-fifths, which included Paris, was occupied by the German military. The southern two-fifths came under a nominally "free" government known as the Vichy Government because of its location in the city of Vichy. To ensure the cooperation of the Vichy Government, Hitler retained more than a million French prisoners of war as hostages.

About 300,000 Jews lived in France at the start of World War II, but the numbers had swelled with refugees from other countries. On July 17, the Vichy Government decreed that non-native Jews could not work in Vichy France. On August 3, it passed anti-Jewish racial laws.

Gurs, in Vichy France, had been established to take in political refugees and soldiers fleeing the Spanish Civil War. After France fell to Germany, Gurs became the dumping place for German Jews—labeled "enemy aliens"—and French political prisoners who opposed the German occupation. The conditions were grim. In 1940–1941, 800 prisoners died of disease.

The French would continue to send Jews and political prisoners to Gurs, St. Cyprien, and other concentration camps in France. Many of the prisoners died in these camps or were eventually deported to extermination camps in Germany. In all, 18,000 of the 22,000 people who passed through or died at Gurs and St. Cyprien were Jewish.

11

Finding Shelter

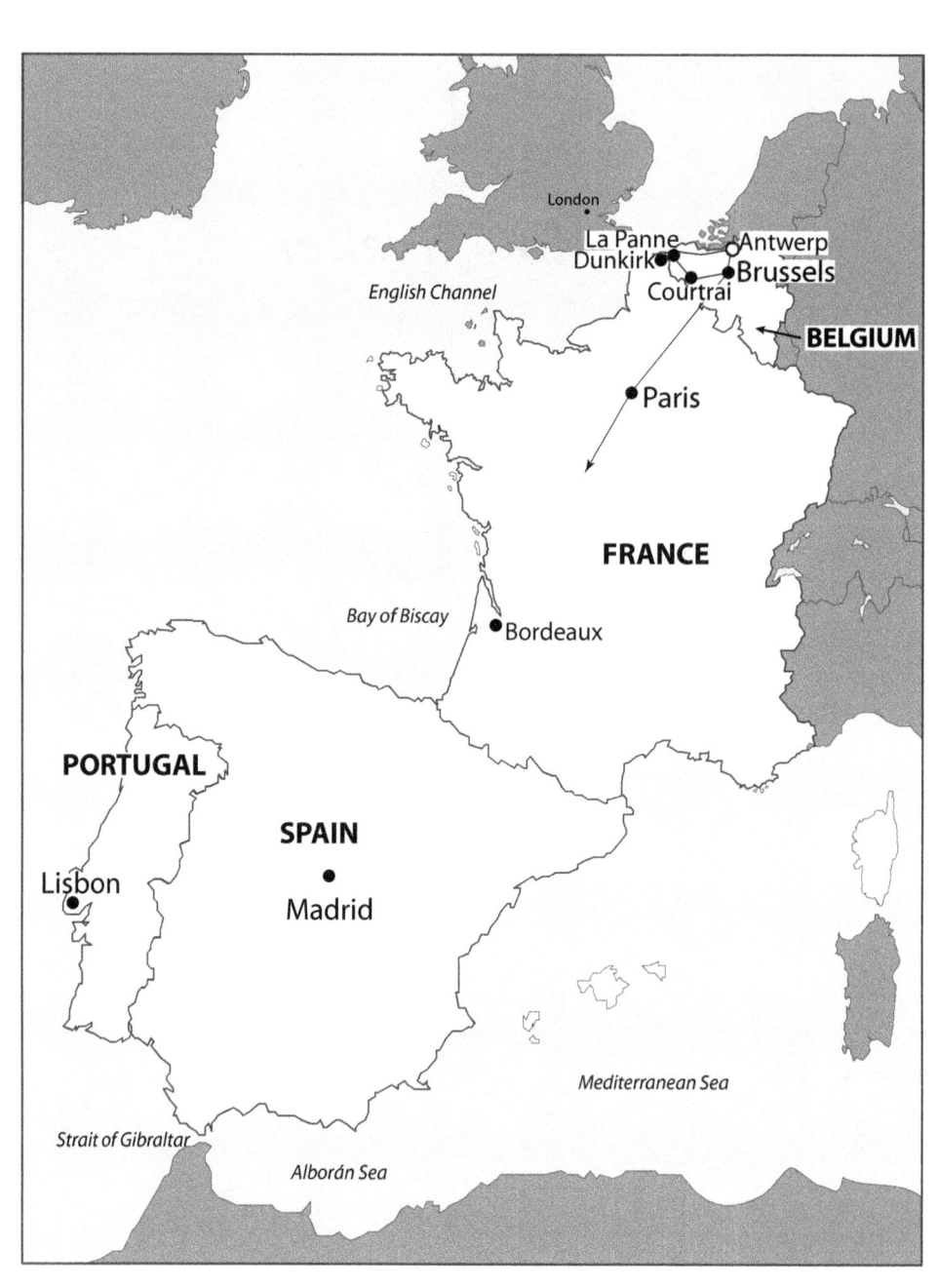

It seemed clear that we needed to leave France—to leave both the occupied area and the so-called Free Zone, which was under the control of the puppet government in Vichy. Italy had come down on the side of the Germans, but Spain, while sympathetic to the Nazis because Hitler had helped Franco during the Spanish Civil War, was maintaining its neutrality. Perhaps we could find a way through Spain to some distant shore. Our first goal, though, was to get out from beneath the iron fist of the Germans.

We set out from Paris, once again hitchhiking. There was much activity on the roads as we traveled southwest toward Bordeaux, a city near the Free Zone that would put us closer to Spain. Hundreds of other refugees, most of them Jewish, had the same idea.

That evening, while the summer sun was still above the horizon, we were deposited by our latest ride on the side of a country road and admonished to find a place to hide before curfew fell. The lowering sun washed the big stone farm houses and barns in a mellow light. We looked around, wondering where to go, when we saw an army truck rumbling toward us. The German army again! We hurried off the road and crept toward the closest farm buildings. The house and barn were joined in one large, long structure. Sheets and undergarments flapped from a clothes line, but no one moved in the yard. Maurice heaved a tall barn door open a crack and motioned me through. The rank smell of animals stung my nose. A cow lowed, and I saw the dim shapes of a couple of sheep who turned large liquid eyes on us as we passed on our way toward the dark rear of the building where straw had been forked into a heap. We unfurled our coats on the prickly pile and lay down. I dug into the pocket of my coat and pulled out some bread. Maurice produced cheese. We munched quietly, wishing we had water, and finally fell into a fitful sleep.

The next day, we continued our journey to Bordeaux. We arrived several days later and found it filled with German soldiers. This made us nervous, so we decided to leave as soon as possible, heading for Pau, a city closer to the French-Spanish border. The next bus to Pau left at midnight.

29. We found refuge in a barn as we fled to Bordeaux.

Finding Shelter

—We'll take two tickets, please.
—Do you have a permit?
—To buy tickets?
—No, no. To get into the Free Zone. Don't you know you can't get out of occupied France into Vichy France without a permit? They check at the border.
—Of course I know that! Two tickets please!

But we hadn't known about the permits. My heart sank. What good were the tickets? Maurice, however, refused to be discouraged. We would take our chances. What other choice did we have?

At midnight, we climbed onto a bus packed with men and women who had been working on German fortifications or in other jobs for the German occupiers. They looked tired.

Someone moved over to allow us to sit, and we hunkered down, trying to look inconspicuous. The little carpet bag seemed not to draw attention. I prayed we blended into the crowd of workers.

The bus lumbered out of Bordeaux down the dark road. Maurice and I held hands, but we dared not speak for fear that our Belgian accents would give us away.

After a while, the bus stopped, and we pressed ourselves to the window. The border! Flashlights, strings of barbed wire, soldiers moving in and out of the light.

The bus door swung open and a French border guard climbed the steps. I gripped Maurice's hand tighter. What would they do to us? Take us to the Germans for interrogation or send us directly to Gurs?

The officer said something to the driver, who laughed. Around us, the workers stirred, reaching into coats and purses for their permits.

Suddenly, the officer turned toward the back of the bus. I held my breath. The sound of his voice sent a jolt through my nerves.

—*Tout le monde a ses papiers?*—Does everyone have his papers?

Around us, hands reached into the air, waving permits like

30. The hotel lobby was filled with sleeping refugees.

white flags of surrender. Then almost with one voice, everyone, including Maurice and me, called out.

—*Oui!*

The guard waved a tired hand and stepped off. In a moment, the bus was across the border, into the Free Zone. Hooray! We were free of the Germans!

We arrived in Pau deep in the night and found a hotel. The lobby was filled with people stretched out on the floor and draped over furniture, tossing and snoring. Grateful to be indoors, we settled down as comfortably as we could, and as quietly, still not daring to speak.

Pau, on high bluffs facing the Pyrenees, was not close enough to the French-Spanish border, so we boarded yet another bus the next day and continued on to Lourdes, famous among Catholics for its healing waters and miracles of renewal.

Lourdes was a captivating city of stone buildings and broad plazas. I would have loved to stay and soak in its waters, but the Pyrenees beckoned in the distance. We had decided that crossing the Pyrenees would be the safest way into Spain. Surely the long, meandering border was too broad and difficult to be patrolled thoroughly.

Lourdes was so full of tourists and refugees that we weren't concerned about our accents. We bought maps of the countryside and pored over them. The shortest route, it seemed, would be from Lourdes to something called the Cirque de Gavarnie. (Neither of us was sure what a cirque was.) From the Cirque de Gavarnie, it was just a few miles to the Spanish border.

Deciding we needed to take a closer look at the route, we pretended to be tourists and rented two donkeys. Pressing our heels into their fat sides, we urged the donkeys out of the city.

First, we passed through a village called Gavarnie. Then we followed a river upstream through a valley edged in rolling hills. The valley broadened, revealing a wall of rock forming part of a circle. Now we understood that "Cirque" referred to the circle of wall. It rose up at the end of the valley to such a height that I gasped. Water thundered down the rock. Snow rimmed its top edge. How could we climb over *that*?

But I was not discouraged for long. A group of hikers we passed answered our anxious inquiries cheerfully, pointing out the path they had taken up the side and over the top. Though the Pyrenees' rocky cliffs and snowy tops looked daunting, we were sure we could climb them; with our spirits lifted, we rode the donkeys back to Lourdes.

We spent some time purchasing a few more supplies.

—We'll need a Spanish dictionary.

Maurice and I spoke many languages (I spoke French in school, German at home, Flemish on the streets; at school I had studied English, Greek, and Latin), but neither of us knew Spanish.

—And what about water?

—We can drink from the streams. The map shows lots of streams.

—And food.

—What kind of food? I mean, how will we carry it?

We needed something that we could carry in our pockets. We strolled around the city, talking.

—Look!

We had stopped outside a store. An elderly man with a poodle on a leash was stooped over on the pavement outside, feeding hard, brown biscuits to his dog.

—That's it!

—That's what?

—What we can take with us to eat!

—Dog biscuits?

—Think how practical they are! They won't crumble or spoil. They cost almost nothing....

—I don't know.... Dog biscuits? Okay, okay. If it's good enough for a French poodle....

Dog biscuits! But at that moment they didn't seem so important. Shortly, we thought, we would be in Spain and on our way to freedom.

31. We surveyed the Cirque de Gavarnie before setting out to cross the Pyrenees.

12
Over the Mountains

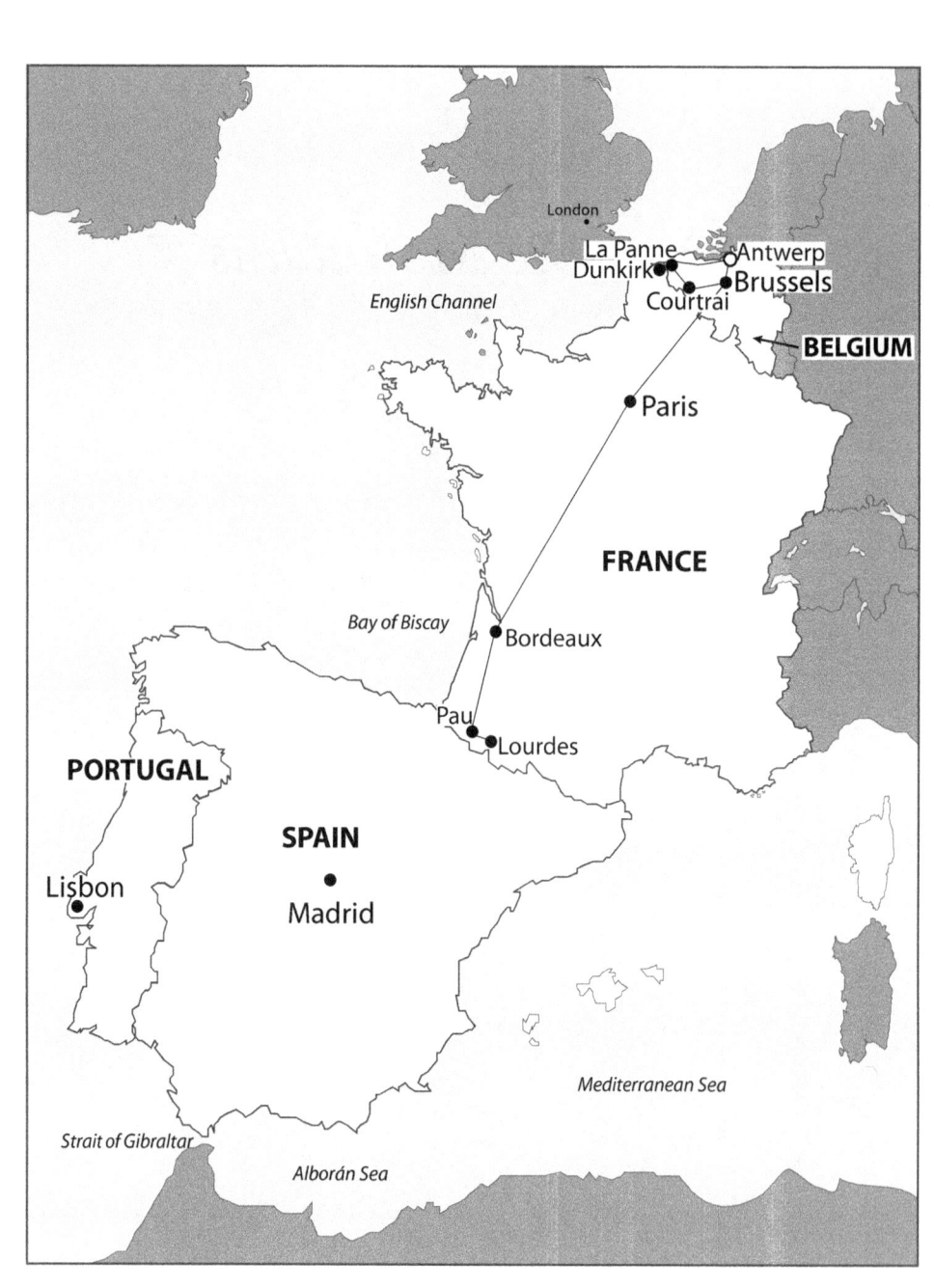

Maurice touched my shoulder.

—Ida, it's 4:30.

I woke with a start, for a moment remembering the shriek of Stukas and the thud of anti-aircraft guns that had awakened me at that same hour on our wedding night. Of course this night was quieter, except for Maurice whispering for me to wake up and the soft snores and murmurs from the other refugees huddled along the hotel hallway. A bulb glowed from a sconce on the wall near the water closet, casting a yellow light on the sleeping forms.

I sat up on the carpet and stretched the knots from my neck and back. Surreptitiously, I touched my bra where the remains of our $80 were pinned. Rising, I straightened my skirt and blouse; the skirt's hem hung loose, and the blouse was missing a button, but there was little I could do about them. I picked up the jacket I had used for a pillow and put it on. Pitiful clothes for hiking over mountains, but they were all I had.

Maurice handed me four dog biscuits.

—The dictionary?

He patted his pocket, then reached for my hand.

Prone figures were draped across the chairs and sofas in the lobby. The air was faintly pungent with sweat.

In a moment we were out the door, which fortunately had not been locked. The streets were dark, and no lights fell from windows that were open to catch the cool morning air. We listened for a moment to the silence, then began walking quickly and quietly through the streets. There was no point in waking anyone and arousing suspicion.

Soon the pavement gave way to dirt and we found ourselves at the edge of town, passing the last hotel, and onto the road to Gavarnie. We whispered as we walked. Now and then we passed farm houses. We were afraid the farmers, rising soon to milk their cows, would wonder at our presence.

The trail rose and fell as it passed through the valley. On either side of us, the rugged foothills stood like black sentinels against the blue-black sky.

A few lights were on in the houses at Gavarnie, so we stepped lightly along the edge of the town and drifted ghostlike toward the cirque. At last the Cirque de Gavarnie appeared before us, a massive black wall in the pre-dawn light. We could hear the din of the distant waterfalls that spilled down its face.

Maurice turned to me and smiled. I shared his excitement. This was the beginning, the way out, our escape. No one would think to look for us here, and once we got into Spain, we would really be free.

We were bursting with confidence as we crossed the valley floor and approached the path we had found the day before. Slowly we began to climb.

When we reached the top of the cirque, the view stopped us. What stretched before us—the peaks lit now with the first light of morning, the valleys still deep in shadow—seemed interminable, vast. How would we ever cross it? But what choice did we have? We could not go back; there was nothing to go back to.

How to describe the following hours, dragging ourselves up steep rocky paths and across broad glacial valleys. We climbed and climbed and climbed and still the mountains rose before us. The sun moved from our left to our right, as we put one foot in front of the other, the soles of our feet aching in our city shoes, the muscles in our thighs quivering.

When we found water spilling down a rock wall, we dipped our hands in and drank. The water was so cold, it made our hands numb, but it refreshed us as the dog biscuits could not. They crumbled tastelessly in our mouths, but they did their duty and filled our stomachs.

Maurice and I had no experience with mountains, and the map had somehow made the distances seem small. We had no idea that a distance of a few miles over a mountain range could take three or four times as long as it might take to stroll along a river in flat Belgium. There are many places to cross the Pyrenees, but in our ignorance, Maurice and I had chosen a difficult route. While the Pyrenees as a whole have an average height of 4,000 feet, our route over the mountains rose to 10,000 feet.

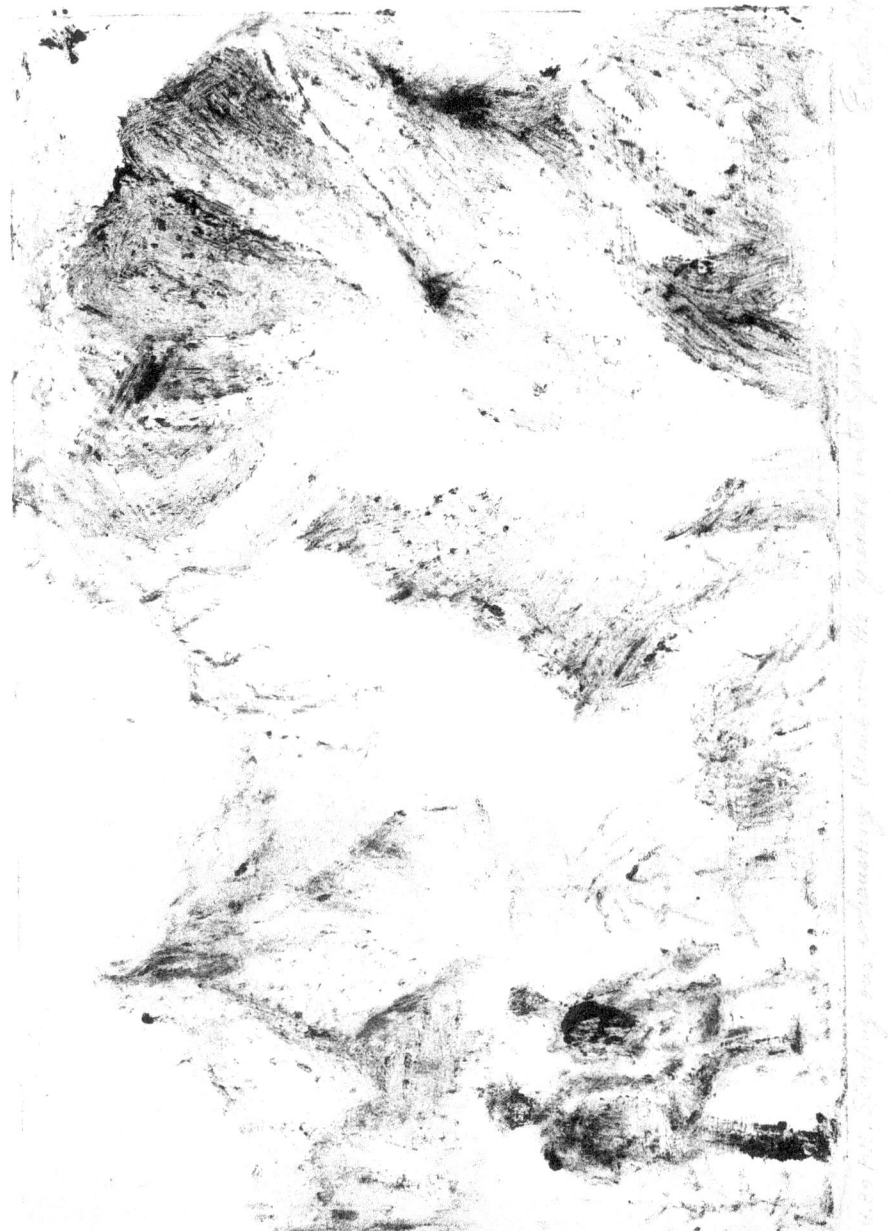

32. We started our exhausting climb before dawn.

As night engulfed us, we stumbled along by feel, picking our way carefully over the uneven ground. Our pace slowed as much from exhaustion as from the darkness. We both longed to lie down and sleep, but we had only our thin jackets for warmth. Unsaid but understood as the air grew colder was the danger of lying down and not waking up.

Sometime in the evening, we crossed from France into Spain, but there was nothing to mark the place. Eventually we began a downward climb into a valley edged with steep, low mountains beside a roaring river.

Near midnight a shout startled us.

—*Alto!*

We froze in the sudden illumination of a flashlight. Several shadowy figures moved behind it.

—*Quienes son ustedes?*

Maurice fumbled for the Spanish-French dictionary, but without light, it was useless. We stood for a moment, uncertain what to do.

The men strode toward us. There were two of them, soldiers, their field-gray uniforms tucked into tall boots, pistols strapped to black belts.

—*De donde vienen?*

Maurice and I shook our heads, not understanding, and called out in French.

—*Nous sommes belges!*—We are Belgian!

The flashlight dropped from our faces. The men stood in front of us, talking rapidly.

—*No comprendo!*—I don't understand!

The flashlight came up to our faces again. I blinked against the light. It dropped once more, and the man said something to me, his voice softer. He took my arm, his touch gentle, and said something rapidly.

—They want us to go with them.

—We're in Spain!

—I don't think I can go another step!

But we did have to walk farther. The soldiers escorted us down the valley. Ahead the lights of a small village winked from a few crude buildings and church ruins made of gray stone slabs. This was San Nicolas de Bujaruelo. The faint path we were on soon changed into a rough dirt road.

The soldiers took us to a house. We entered a room with a single table and several chairs. In the light from oil lamps scattered around the room, Maurice looked at his watch.

—We've been walking twenty hours!

Several other soldiers looked up from their places at the table. Two were smoking cigarettes and a third slapped cards onto the table and stared at them intensely, playing solitaire.

We were ushered to seats, and a conversation ensued among us, with Maurice and me passing the dictionary back and forth and the Spanish soldiers speaking first to each other and then to us.

Finally, it became clear: They did not know what to do with us. The sergeant in charge spoke to one of the soldiers, and we understood that the soldier was being sent by horse to a town a couple of hours away to ask a superior for instructions.

The soldiers brought us mugs of water, and we drank thirstily, trying to rinse the gritty remnants of dog biscuit from our mouths. After a while one of them appeared with plates of eggs, burnt at the edges and swimming in brown olive oil. The oil was rank, and I wondered how long they had been using the same grease to fry their eggs. Of the many strange foods we had been forced to eat on our travels—including dog biscuits!—this was by far the worst. But our hunger urged us on, and we forced the eggs down.

When we had finished eating, our hosts led us back into the street. After a short walk, we were invited into a house and given a room with a double bed. We fell into it without undressing and were asleep in minutes.

The next morning, we were brought back to the office of the border patrol. The soldier who had been sent away the night before had returned. Slowly, with much passing of the dictionary, we learned that Franco had an agreement with Hitler. No men of military age—between 16 and 40—were to be allowed into Spain.

The soldiers gestured to me.

—*La señora puede pasar, pero el señor, no!*

I could remain, but Maurice would have to go back. I fought tears and shook my head. No! I wasn't staying without Maurice! He put his arm around me, his full lips pinched, his face pale.

The sergeant shrugged and raised his hands, palms forward, and lifted his chin slightly in a gesture that said, I am sorry, I have no choice.

He rapped out an order and one of the men disappeared and returned with sandwiches, some sort of meat wrapped in bread. I took one and thrust it into my pocket, trying to feel grateful.

The sergeant escorted us out of the building. A horse-drawn carriage stood in front. Holding back sobs, I climbed into the back seat. Maurice followed and quietly held me close. The sergeant and the card player climbed into the front.

The carriage rumbled out of the village, so peaceful and innocent on that summer morning. I could not bring myself to look behind us as we wound our way up again into the foothills.

The soldiers did not take us back exactly the way we had come, but rather brought us along a road that took us closer to France. Finally the car stopped. Reluctantly we stepped out onto the dirt road.

The sergeant frowned, his eyebrows almost meeting, his face stern in a way it had not been before.

—*No regresen!*

I shook my head, confused. His demeanor frightened me; Maurice's grip tightened on my hand.

Reaching down to his waist, the sergeant unsnapped the leather holster that kept his gun in place. His hand circled the handle and he pulled it out. He gestured towards us with the gun.

—*Si regresan, les vamos a disparar!*

We needed no translation—If you come back, we will shoot you.

33. The Spanish patrol forced us back across the border.

Maurice turned and looked up the road we were expected to travel. He sighed deeply, glanced at me and, with the faintest of smiles, began walking. I bit my lip to keep the tears in check and followed.

It was incomprehensible that after all we had been through, we should be turned away. Where could we go now? What country would let us in?

13

Night in a Strange Hotel

Since Maurice and I had set out from Antwerp, we had experienced discomfort, physical pain, and breath-strangling fear; now we were faced with despair, the same despair we had felt at La Panne. We had not expected the Spanish to let us in easily, but we had not allowed ourselves to think of failing.

Our return journey to Lourdes was shorter because the Spanish border guards had taken us closer to the French border and set us down on a better road, but we were still forced to walk for many hours across rugged land.

On swollen feet and aching thighs, we found our way back to Lourdes. Now we no longer passed for healthy tourists; we hobbled into town like invalids. We found a room in a hostel and collapsed on the bed. For the next three days, we barely moved, venturing out only for food and drink. My feet were swollen to twice their size. We could have used a few of those crutches hanging all over the caves of St. Bernadette, left there by people who believed they had been cured.

When we began to feel better—and our feet had almost returned to their normal sizes—we did the only thing we could do: We took out the map and explored other possibilities.

After our experiences in La Panne, we had no stomach for traveling west, to the sea, so we decided to try our luck in Toulouse.

We bought tickets at the railway station and arrived in Toulouse in the late evening. To our dismay, the city was packed with refugees. We wandered along boulevards and down narrow streets, searching for a hostel. My feet and legs had not completely recovered and began to voice their unhappiness in painful ways. Around midnight, we were ready to give up when we found ourselves standing before a small hotel whose large windows threw light onto the sidewalk. Maurice opened the door for me and we forced ourselves to the counter, leaning on it wearily.

Perhaps it was a loud sigh or the sound of exhausted feet dragging across the tile floor, but a thin man who had been snoozing in a chair in the lobby jerked to his feet.

—Do you have a room?

—You want a room *here?*

—Yes, if you have one. Or at least let us sleep in the lobby. We've been on our feet for hours.

We looked around the empty lobby. It was strange not to see it filled with sleeping figures as so many other hotel lobbies were. It did not bode well for us if they were turning away refugees. The man pursed his lips and tilted his head, surveying us.

—*Oui, Oui.* I think I have a room. But you must be out by seven in the morning.

—Gladly, anything. We agree to anything.

The man did not shove a registry at us but instead picked up a key from one of the pigeon holes behind the desk and handed it to us, describing where we could find the room.

Bleary eyed, we stumbled our way down the darkened hall and unlocked the door. Maurice was even more exhausted than I was.

—No lights, please. I just want to sleep.

—Look, it has a bath and shower!

—You go ahead, I'm going to sleep!

I filled the tub with hot water and sank into it. Oh, the luxury! It had been weeks since I had bathed. I scrubbed my hair, then toweled off. In the darkened bedroom I slipped into bed beside my sleeping husband, feeling more refreshed than I had since leaving Antwerp. Shortly, I joined Maurice in sleep.

The telephone woke us in the morning.

—It's six thirty! You must be out by seven.

I opened my eyes and heard Maurice laughing beside me. I turned to see Maurice with his head thrown back staring at the ceiling. I followed his gaze and was startled to see two figures—Maurice and me!—looking down at us on the bed. I sat up and looked at the walls. All around us, on every wall and across the ceiling were mirrors.

—We're in a....

—A bordello!

We scrambled out of bed, still laughing, to glory in the luxury of the bathroom. Just before seven, we found our way back to the lobby. The man from the night before was busy behind the desk.

—Sorry to rouse you. But you see....
—We're grateful to have been able to sleep here. Thank you.
—There are coffee and rolls on that table, if you like. By the way, you might want to go to the marketplace. Many of the refugees are gathering there. Maybe you can learn something useful.

We thanked him, had a quick breakfast, and strolled out into the sunshine to the marketplace.

While the city had seemed filled with refugees the night before, the marketplace was strangely quiet. Women with baskets over their arms prodded the fruit and sniffed the cheeses, but there was a striking absence of people with the shocked or weary faces we had come to associate with refugees.

We were just deciding what we should do next when a voice spoke Maurice's name. The tone was that of someone who wants to call out urgently but has learned restraint. We looked around. Coming toward us along the wooden booths were childhood friends of Maurice's—François and another man whose name I have since forgotten. They greeted us warmly. We laughed when we told them where we had spent the night, but the conversation quickly turned to more serious matters.

—You were fortunate they didn't chase you out earlier.
—What do you mean?
—The French police just came through. They rounded up all the foreigners—anyone without a permit—and sent them to Gurs and St. Cyprien.
—It's not a good idea to be standing out here. Come to our room. We are in a little hotel down this street.

The two had been sharing a bed in the small room, but they turned it over to Maurice and me and threw the mattress on the floor for themselves. We relaxed on our beds and talked. They tried to dissuade us from continuing our journey.

—You'll end up in Gurs.
—No, you'll see. We'll get out...somehow.
—Somehow? Look, I have a letter from my sister in Antwerp. Read it. She says it is not so bad. The Germans are friendly, everything is calm.

34. We pleaded with the refugees not to return to Belgium.

—The Germans can't be trusted! What about all those stories we heard from people who ran away from Germany before the invasion? What about *Kristallnacht*?

—Well, we're tired of hiding, and we're running out of money. Tomorrow there will be buses in the marketplace that will take us home.

—What do you mean—us? What buses?

—I mean us, the refugees. The French are providing us with a free ride home.

—No, you can't go back!

—Where should we go? Where will you go?

— Anyplace away from Europe! We'll get visas to….

—I've heard that there are consulates in Marseilles giving out visas.

—Really? Which ones?

—I don't know, but we met some people who were going there.

—Then we will go there too!

We tried our best to dissuade Maurice's friends from returning to Antwerp, but they were as adamant about returning as we were about running away. The next morning we parted ways. Maurice and I set out on foot toward the south coast and the French port city of Marseilles.

14

Visa Maze

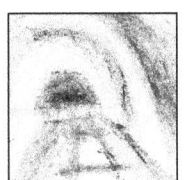

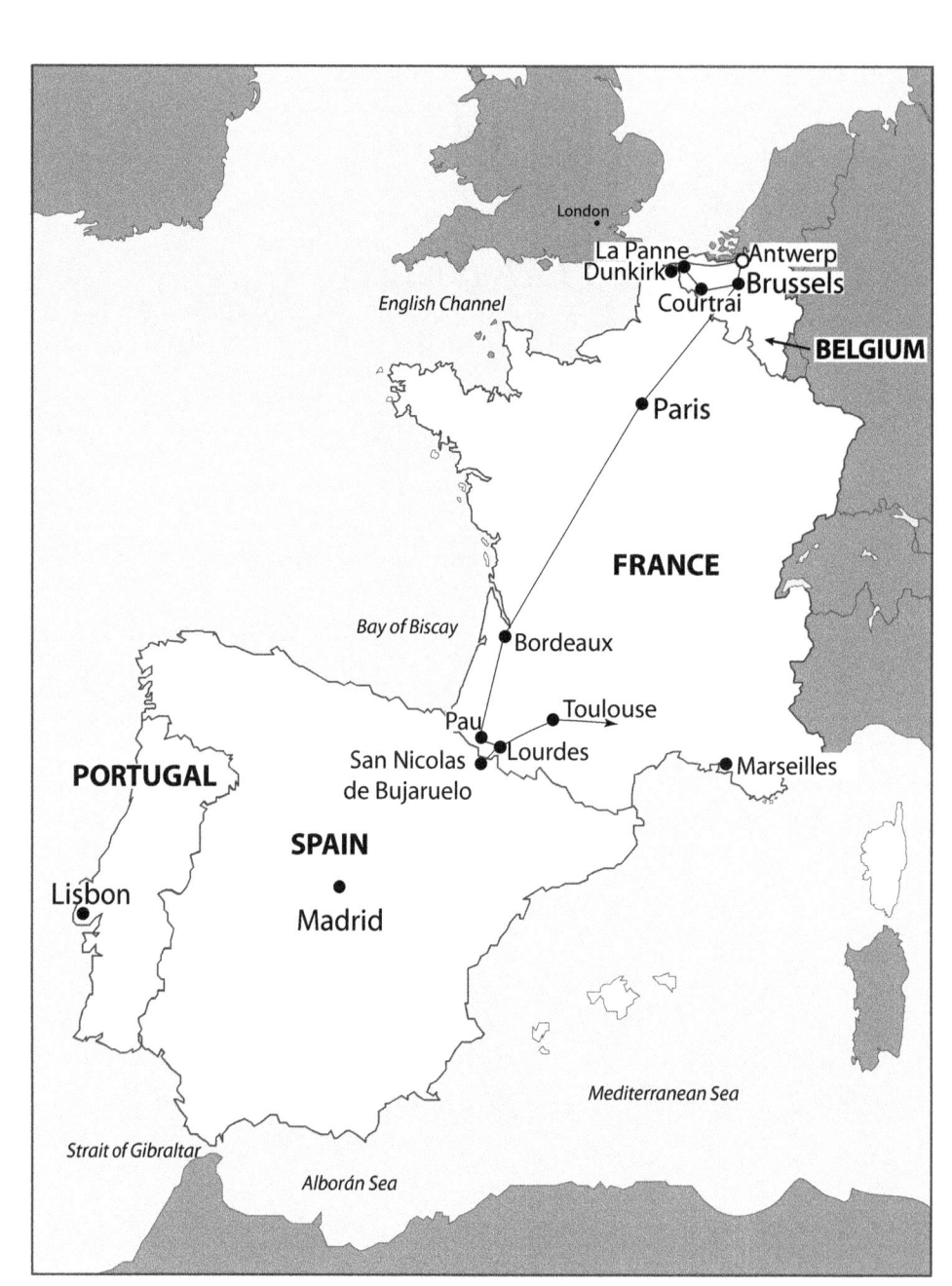

Outside of Toulouse, we spent the first night huddled with other refugees in a long, dark train tunnel. The next morning we hiked to a nearby village and caught the train to Marseilles.

The station was mobbed with people as we stepped out onto the platform. It was impossible to walk side by side, so I strode ahead of Maurice, veering through the crowd and trusting he was close behind.

Around us, men and women were moving briskly, some looking over their shoulders, others with their heads down. There was something about the crowd that made me uneasy. Suddenly, on either side of me, two French policemen pressed through the crowd. My pace picked up; I kept walking right past them.

—*Monsieur!*

I heard Maurice respond behind me.

—*Oui?*

Heart pounding, I wondered what to do—slow down? Stop? I kept walking. One of the policemen barked a command.

—*Vos papiers, s'il vous plait!*—Your papers, please!

—*Oui, mais ma femme! Je vais la perdre dans cette foule!*—Yes, but my wife! I'm going to lose her in this crowd!

—*Ah, vous parlez français! Vous etes français?*—Oh, you speak French! You are French?

—*Bien sur! Ma femme …!*—Of course. My wife …!

And miraculously, they let him through!

A moment later he caught my elbow and steered me toward the station coffee shop. Hands shaking, hearts pounding—as much from the excitement as from the hurried retreat we had just made—we ordered sandwiches and coffee.

Through the coffee shop window, we began to see a pattern in the movement of the police. When a train arrived, the police would suddenly appear. They harassed the disembarking passengers, then disappeared until the arrival of the next train. As soon as we picked up on their movements, we waited for a train to leave, watched the French police melt away with the crowd, and then walked quickly from the station. Later, we learned that some

35. We slept in an abandoned tunnel with other refugees.

prisoners had escaped from the prison at St. Cyprien and the police were trying to track them down.

We were not the only refugees who hoped to get visas to another country. It seemed every consulate had lines snaking from its doors and down long city blocks. From the way people slouched against the walls or sat on the sidewalks, we could tell they had been waiting for hours.

We wandered through the city from consulate to consulate, questioning those waiting as to whether they thought this foreign country or that foreign country would let us in. No one knew for sure, of course. They were living on rumors just as we were.

Rumors finally led us to the Chinese consulate.

—China!

—Well, it's not Germany.

We asked if the Chinese visas were valid.

—Who cares? They will get you out of France! Look, with the Chinese visa, you can get a transit visa to some port like Lisbon, and then you can get a different visa to the United States or Palestine or wherever.

Upon further questioning, we discovered that the Chinese visa—which we assumed was not valid—would indeed allow us to obtain a transit visa to Portugal. With that transit visa, we could be granted a Spanish transit visa good for forty-eight hours. We would get into Spain somehow and then travel through Spain to Portugal. The Portuguese transit visas were good for two weeks. Surely in that time we could find a country that would take us!

We decided, then, to try for visas from the Chinese, Portuguese, and Spanish consulates. It was a simple decision to make, but not so simple to execute. We rose at four in the morning to find a place in line at the Chinese consulate, then waited all day and into the next before we finally reached an official. After getting the Chinese visa, we convinced the Portuguese consulate to give us a two-week transit visa to Portugal so we could catch a ship to China. With the Portuguese transit visa in hand, we were able to convince the Spanish consulate officials to allow us to

36. In Marseilles, we waited 48 hours for each of our visas.

travel through their country to Lisbon. By the time we left the Spanish consulate, our spirits were lifted, but we were too exhausted to celebrate. We hurried to the bus station to buy tickets for the French-Spanish border. Along the way, at the French town of Perpignan, we met some acquaintances who told us that we would need an exit visa to leave the Free Zone, which was beginning to look less "free" all the time.

—What! Why didn't anyone tell us this? How do we get one?

—Ha! It's impossible! The French aren't going to give an exit visa to someone who is in the country illegally. They will ship you off to a camp if you try.

—Then what will we do? We've already tried crossing on our own.

—You can pay a smuggler to help you across. They are operating along the border.

—How much would that cost?

—Thousands of francs.

We had very little of our original money left—nowhere near enough. I turned disheartened to Maurice. What could we do now? But Maurice's spirits could not be dampened. He put his arm around me and smiled.

—We'll go to the border anyway. Maybe we will meet a nice person.

Maybe we'll meet a nice person! It seemed so much to pin our hopes on, but what alternative did we have?

The next morning we boarded a bus for the French border town of Le Perthus, burying ourselves in the back of the bus and keeping silent. When the vehicle squealed to a halt outside the French border station, with its long red and white poles crossing the road, we saw a French policeman rifling through the papers of the passengers in the front of the bus. I tugged at Maurice's arm, and he nodded. None of the other passengers commented as we quietly stood and exited through the rear door of the bus.

Our clothes were casual, and all we were carrying was a small bag. We must have appeared very much like locals taking a morning walk. We veered left and forced ourselves to take a leisurely pace away from the bus. All the time, however, our minds were working furiously. We're at the border! How would we get across? So close!

We walked a few blocks along a sidewalk lined with shabby stucco buildings, turning our heads away when we saw a couple of Spanish soldiers march by on the other side of the street. Shortly, we came to a little grocery store. Wooden bins sagging with oranges and melons stood in front of the open door.

We decided to buy some bread and cheese while we thought about how to cross the border. In the dimly lit store, the proprietor was arranging cans on a shelf, the frayed sleeves of his shirt pulled back to reveal plump arms. He turned as we entered.

—*Bonjour! Est-ce que je peux vous aider?*—Hello. Can I help you?

When we responded to his cheerful greeting, he did not seem surprised by our accent. In fact, something about him seemed sympathetic. Perhaps, just perhaps....

My heart beat fast and Maurice grabbed my hand.

—*S'il vous plaît, nous voulons aller en Espagne.*—Please, we'd like to go to Spain.

The man raised his eyebrows and seemed surprised by the question.

—Spain? That's easy! Just cross the street and you are in Spain.

Of course! That explained the Spanish patrol we had just seen! Paying the shopkeeper with a few of our remaining francs and with our effusive thanks, we quickly walked across the street. Our pace was more hurried now. We could hardly believe our good luck. Maurice had been right, we had met a nice person!

On the Spanish side of the street, as we approached the place where we had left the bus, we noticed a small building with the red-and-yellow Spanish flag whipping from a pole on the roof. The building stood beside a bridge. We stepped up to the Spanish soldier on duty. I glanced back at the French border guard a few dozen feet behind us, a frown on his face, and his hand gripped tightly around his pistol. But what could he do?

37. Our hearts leapt as we crossed the border into Spain.

I turned back to see the Spanish guard checking Maurice's passport. I had no passport of my own, since we had added my name to his after our wedding, when we had returned to Antwerp from La Panne. The guard nodded, then took the paper visas Maurice offered to him.

Handing back the papers, the guard stepped aside. We had done it!

Jubilantly, we almost skipped across the bridge where, to our delight, we saw the same bus we had sneaked off an hour earlier, its engine running. Grinning, we climbed aboard and found our seats at the back once again.

We had settled back, feeling elated and relaxed and thinking of our next stop, Barcelona, when the bus suddenly shook with the heavy steps of someone charging down the length of the aisle. A man threw himself toward us so fast, we did not have time to react.

15

Escape

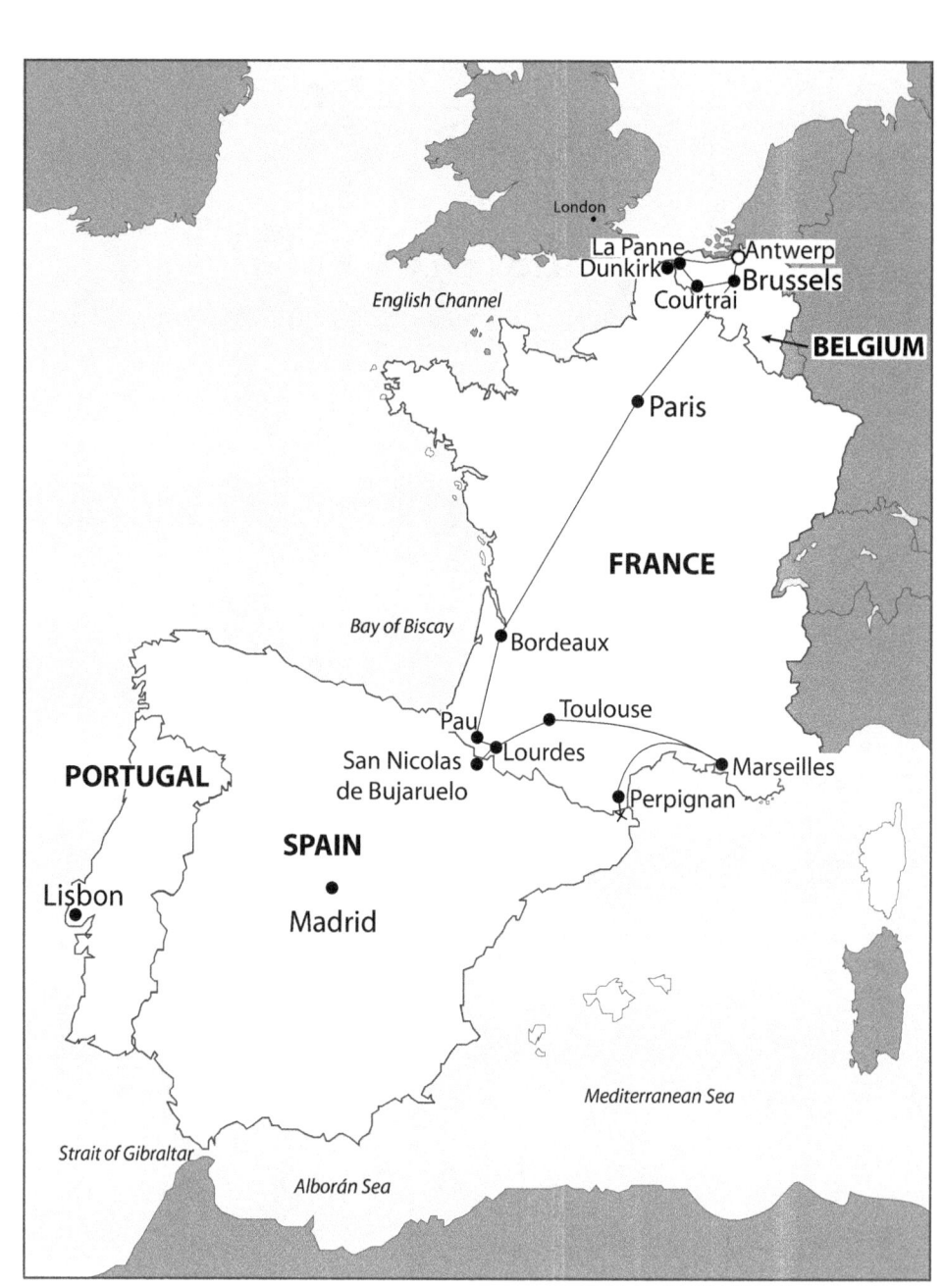

Terrified, Maurice and I watched helplessly as the young man flung himself down onto the bench seat beside me. He gasped for breath at first, unable to speak. When he caught his breath, we were as surprised as we had been frightened to hear him greet us in Yiddish.

—*Sholem Aleykhem!*—Peace be with you!

—*Aleykhem Sholem!* You scared us! What were you doing? You ran at us like a crazy man!

—I ran like the wind! I saw you get off at the border. I was on this bus, too. I guessed you were like me—no exit visa.

—But how did you…?

—I told the driver to keep my luggage because I was going to get across no matter what! As I was going toward the front door of the bus, the French *gendarme* asked me for my visa, so I ran.

—You *what?*

—I ran for my life! Before he knew what was happening, before he could draw his pistol, I had reached the Spanish guardhouse, showed him my Spanish transit visa, and just kept going. I wasn't giving anyone time to think, and here I am!

Oh, how we laughed with him! We laughed and cried and talked all the way to Barcelona, excited and happy and relieved to be out of France and closer to freedom and safety.

The bus lumbered into Barcelona as the sun was sinking. We stepped off with the young man, wondering where we would stay in this strange city, with its large, shabby buildings of gray stone. But our luck held, for suddenly a voice rang out through the bus station.

—*Alguien para el hotel Sholem Aleykhem?*—Anyone for Hotel *Sholem Aleykhem*?

We laughed. *Sholem Aleykhem* is a Yiddish phrase probably only Jews would understand.

The voice belonged to a volunteer from the local Jewish community waiting at the station to offer shelter to Jewish refugees. We were fed and given a small but comfortable room for the night. The next morning, someone took us to the train station

38. In Barcelona, a local Jewish organization gave us shelter.

and gave us sandwiches for the journey. We boarded a train for Madrid. From there, we would travel on to Lisbon in Portugal. But we had to hurry—our Spanish visa was good for just forty-eight hours.

Our meager francs bought us tickets in third class where we crowded onto wooden benches beside Spanish men, women, and children. The mass of humanity raised the car's temperature, so the windows were left open. The coal-burning engine spewed black soot back at us as we wove in and out of a seemingly endless string of tunnels. By the time we arrived in Madrid, our faces and clothes—even my blonde hair—were as black as pitch.

Our train had arrived late at the station. We were disappointed to find that we had missed the connection to Lisbon. Never mind, we thought, we had enough time to get there before our Spanish transit visas expired. We fished handkerchiefs from our bag, wiped off our faces as best we could, and made our way to a large outdoor market, looking for lodging as we walked.

Our luck continued to hold. We ran into some people we had met in Perpignan who were well-to-do and could afford to stay in a fancy hotel for a few days. We asked them for the use of their bathroom to clean up, and they invited us to stay with them. It was heaven to watch the black water pooling in the sink gradually run clear as I washed my hair. Afterward, we asked where we might find something to eat.

—Bread and cheese. That's all we need.
—Well, don't try to buy bread. It's rationed!
—Then what...?
—Cake!

So we ate cake, thinking of Marie Antoinette's famous words.

The next morning, we bid our new friends goodbye and climbed back onto the coal-fueled train, ready to finish our journey through Spain. Our visas for Portugal were good for just two weeks, but so many good things had happened in the last few days, so many people had helped us. Surely, real freedom could not be more than a fortnight away.

16

Hopes Dashed

M aurice and I rode into Lisbon's railway station as exhilarated as climbers reaching the peak of Everest. It was September 13, 1940, a little over two months since we had left Antwerp.

We rose from our seat as the brakes shrieked and the train jerked to a stop. A black cloud of soot dissipated against the once-white walls of the grand stone building. Maurice grinned at me.

—A free country at last! Things will be easy now!

My usual sober outlook gave way to Maurice's eternal optimism. Yes! Many countries had consulates in Lisbon and in Portugal's second-largest port city, Porto. We had heard that some people had already emigrated successfully. Surely our turn would come soon.

And look how easy staying in Lisbon would be! After we passed easily through customs, a representative of a Jewish refugee organization was waiting on the platform to direct us to a refugee center where we were furnished with a room. There was a toilet down the hall, though, of course, no bath. A soup kitchen would serve us a midday meal. For advice and assistance, we could turn to the Hebrew Immigration Aid Society (HIAS) and the American Jewish Joint Distribution Committee, organizations that were both active in helping Jews in Portugal. We learned that HIAS would provide us with a ticket on a passenger ship once we got a visa to another country, which we would need since we were convinced our Chinese visas were invalid—and anyway, there were no boats to China from Lisbon.

* * *

The line at the soup kitchen snaked past tables of soup, spicy fried fish and meat, vegetables swimming in olive oil, and hearty loaves of bread, cheerfully served by members of the local Portuguese Jewish community. As we waited, we exchanged names and news with other refugees, some of whom we knew from Antwerp but all of whom had left Belgium before the Germans attacked. They were full of curiosity about what the country was like under

39. At last we arrived in Lisbon.

the German occupation and whether we had seen loved ones they had left behind. We answered as best we could, and we had our own questions.

—How long do you think it will take to get a visa?

—Who knows? Look at these people here. Most of them have been waiting for months.

—Months? But our visa for Portugal is just a transit visa. It's good for only two weeks!

—Hasn't anyone told you? You must register with the Portuguese police every two weeks. They decide then whether you can stay.

Maurice and I looked at each other, aghast.

—We can be sent back to Belgium?

—Well, it's not so bad. Look, as long as these good people feed us and give us a mattress to sleep on, we aren't a burden on the locals and they'll let us stay.

Some of the elation I had felt coming into Lisbon began to slip, as if I had suddenly skidded backward on an icy spot on Everest. The peak, it seemed, was still elusive.

Maurice, as usual, tried to keep my spirits up.

—You see, Ida, they will let us stay as long as we don't work.

—But one meal a day….

—Then we'll eat a lot! We'll manage. Haven't we managed so far?

We had managed, but while some of our efforts had been brought about by our own bravado—hitching rides with German soldiers in Belgium, bluffing our way past collaborator police in Marseilles—just as much had come down to plain dumb luck. How long would that luck hold?

We decided to begin visiting consulates immediately. Rumors told us that there were several thousand refugees, mostly Jewish, in Portugal—some in Porto but most in Lisbon. They would make our waits at the consulates long, though we hoped not as long as in Marseilles. While we were planning our assault on the consulates, we paced the hilly, twisting streets past big stone buildings, impressive statues to fallen heroes, and tiled or pastel-tinted

40. Jewish refugees crowded the soup kitchen.

façades. We barely gave these things a glance, so focused were we on solving our problems. But now and then we lifted our eyes from the cobbled streets to stare at the squat sandstone castle of St. George dominating the tallest hill, or the blue water of the harbor. It was a beautiful city that in another time we would have loved to explore. When someone told us that it had been completely rebuilt after a devastating earthquake and fires in the eighteenth century, I wondered if we would be able to rebuild our lives so well after the havoc wreaked by this war.

Slowly, our days took on a rhythm—wake in the morning, eat a bit of fruit or bread if we could buy it and, if we were lucky, drink a cup of chicory coffee at a cafe, then begin the rounds of the consulates. At noon, we would stuff ourselves at the soup kitchen and fill our pockets with bread and leftovers for later in the day. At one point, we ran into one of my sister's well-to-do friends—Paula—and I spent afternoons babysitting for her child, her niece, and her nephew to earn a little money for extra meals and necessities. Maurice spent the afternoon in cafes hunting rumors with other refugees.

—What's the news?

—Did you hear about the American consul in Porto? He is not like this one here.

—How so?

—He doesn't look at your affidavits very closely.

—Then we should....

—Too late, you are registered here and they won't let you switch. Too bad. The American consul in Lisbon looks for every excuse to keep from giving us visas.

Oh, how we hated Lisbon's American consul! I don't remember his name or his face, only that he held our lives in his hands and we hated and feared him.

The consul demanded affidavits to show that we would not be a drain on the American economy. Not satisfied with the first affidavits, he insisted that we each have $3,000 in a U.S. bank—a fortune at that time. We learned that in Porto, too, the consul was required to ensure that the refugees could support themselves if they went to the United States. But he allowed refugees to pool their money, present it to him as evidence, and then pass the same money on to the next person. Both the consuls in Porto and Lisbon followed the same rules, but their interpretations made all the difference.

We wrote letter after letter to the United States—to friends, to Maurice's sister Myri (who had been visiting the World's Fair in New York City when the war broke out), and to the widow of his recently deceased brother Simon in Chicago. Everyone willingly sent the documents, which we brought to the U.S. consul, who took them and demanded more.

Unsure of whether we would be able to get into the United States but desperate to escape, we, like others, stood in long lines at other consulates. We tried the consulates of Britain, Mexico, Canada, Argentina, Brazil, and other South American countries, as well as the consulates of several African countries.

Every one we visited had its own reason for refusing us a visa—not enough money or not the right papers or not the right policy. We suspected anti-Semitism played a role in all of this.

Great Britain would take Maurice to fight in its Polish Army, but it would not let me in. Britain closed Palestine to us as well. Cuba would let us in only if we had $3,000 each, which of course we did not have. South Africa was for Dutch citizens only, and the Belgian Congo was open only to Belgians, while we were Polish citizens.

And every two weeks we went to the Portuguese police, our hearts in our hands.

—Please, two more weeks. We almost have our visas to Cuba…to the United States…to Argentina….

One day we heard that Dr. Schwarz of the American Jewish Joint Distribution Committee was looking for five hundred strong young couples to emigrate to the Dominican Republic. Couples with children need not apply. All you had to do was sign a contract to spend five years draining swamps.

—Draining swamps?

—It would be a way out.

—My God, is this our only choice?

—I don't know. We should be getting another letter from the United States any day.

—Let's wait a little longer. Draining swamps…!

* * *

Fall slipped into winter. We kept up our rounds at the consulates, wrapped in our thin jackets against cold winter drizzles. When winter turned to spring, we fanned ourselves in the warm humid air. We shifted to relieve our aching backs, shared hard bread pocketed from the soup kitchen, listened to the stream of stories from our fellow refugees, and waited and waited.

Eventually, Paula and her family boarded a ship for the United States, while Maurice and I were left behind, eating one meal a day and nervously fingering our last few coins.

By spring, we had collected five affidavits vouching for our ability to support ourselves or be supported by friends and family, but the U.S. consul was still not satisfied.

—Yes. These look very good, I'm sure, but you also need affidavits to prove you are not Communists.

—What? Why didn't you tell us this before?

—The rules have changed. It can't be helped.

We choked back our rage. We wanted to ask him—Why are you doing this to us? But we were afraid of his answer: Because you have no money, because we don't want you, because you are Jewish.

And through all this the German army, now with Italy's help, was roaring through Europe. Romania, Greece, Yugoslavia, North Africa. How long before Hitler turned on Spain? How long could tiny Portugal remain neutral?

The rumors that swept the refugee community fed our fever. By the fall of 1940, the Gestapo had started systematically oppressing the Jews in grim but predictable ways. The internment camps began to take on a far more sinister character than that of mere work camps or prisons. The Nazis were swallowing up the Jews of Europe, and the world had closed its doors.

41. Nowhere to go—the world had closed its doors.

17

The Train from Berlin

One day in March, the soup kitchen was alive with gossip as we found our place in line. Had we heard? A train was arriving soon. It carried five hundred women, children, and older men, Jews who had spent months waiting for American visas to emigrate, and still more time waiting for exit visas from Germany and transit visas through Spain and Portugal.

We hurried through our meal and walked up the hill to the train station. Apparently the passengers had been on the sealed train without food or water for two days. It seemed only natural to greet them as they descended onto the platform.

Anxious faces pressed against the windows of the cars as the steam engine huffed into view. We waved and smiled, and after some hesitation, we were rewarded with weary grins. We called greetings as the people disembarked.

—Welcome to Lisbon!

—Thank God! What a nightmare trip we've had!

—Where are you from?

—Berlin. It's terrible there. People shot in the street, hanged. My God, my God.

—But you're here now.

—Yes, safe. It's a miracle, I tell you.

They lugged their valises through the Lisbon streets to a refugee center that could accommodate their large number, and the next day, they went to the American consul to ask for an extension of their visas. Because of all the delays they had experienced in selling their property and obtaining the required papers, their visas for entering the United States were valid for just five more days. There were no ships in the Lisbon harbor to take them, but one was expected shortly. The ocean voyage to the United States took ten days, and if they were granted a one-week extension, they would arrive in New York before their American visas expired.

Two representatives from HIAS flew in from New York and met with the consul. It seemed a simple enough request. One week. Just stamp the papers. Who could refuse?

42. *The sealed train opened, and hundreds of Berlin Jews poured out.*

—They're sending them back.
—How can that be!
—He won't do it. He won't extend the visas.
—I can't believe it! Not back to Berlin!

Nothing could sway the American consul. The Berlin refugees were allowed just two days in Lisbon before they were forced to leave again. They had to return to Berlin.

The station filled with refugees. We watched helplessly as the Berliners shuffled along the platform. Valises bumped against legs and dragged across the floor. How could they lift their feet to reenter those railway cars? How could they bear to move at all?

Maurice and I held each other and watched five hundred human beings go back to—what? Starvation in a ghetto? Slow death in a work camp? Murder by the Gestapo?

Boys in short pants and girls with their hair in braided ringlets looked confused and watched the faces of their mothers and grandparents for signs of how they should react. Old men clutched small hands and kept their heads high so their tears would wash unnoticed into their snowy beards. A mother passed holding her infant tightly to her chest, her fingertips white.

A sob filled my throat and I felt Maurice's body shudder. We were overcome with a deep, impotent rage, chilled by the prospect that our own fate might one day take such a turn.

Around us people began to cry. Soon the platform was filled with men, women, and children moaning and wailing, Maurice and I among them, weeping for these strangers as we had not wept for ourselves through all our trials. It was a terrible noise whose memory sixty years later still fills me with anguish.

Yet for all our cries, it seemed heaven did not hear. The sound drifted forlornly in the spring air, then dissipated with the black soot of the departing train.

43. I wept as the men, women, and children were forced back onto the train.

At the beginning of the war, the United States erected a "paper wall," a bureaucratic maze that prevented all but a relatively few Jewish refugees from entering the country. As expressed in a memo in June of 1940 by Assistant Secretary of State Breckinridge Long, "We can delay and effectively stop for a temporary period of indefinite length the number of immigrants into the United States . . . by simply advising our consuls to put every obstacle in the way and to require additional evidence and to resort to various administrative devices which would postpone and postpone and postpone the granting of the visas."

Thus, most refugees were stonewalled—turned away. This policy continued even after there was clear evidence of Hitler's genocidal policies.

The United States was not the only country denying access to Jewish refugees. Many others found ways to keep them out. In a lesser known incident, over 760 Jewish refugees from Romania paid an exorbitant price to board a ship called the Struma that was supposedly bound for Palestine. The ship turned out to be a cattle ship with one bathroom, no kitchen, and a motor that failed frequently. En route, it stopped in Istanbul, ostensibly to pick up the Palestinian immigration certificates that would be waiting for the passengers. Unfortunately there were no certificates, and Britain pressured Turkey not to allow the ship to pass through the Straits of Bosphorus. Romania would not allow the ship to return home, and Turkey adamantly refused to let a single refugee disembark—not even the children—even though it had run out of fresh water, food, and fuel. The ship was towed some six miles from the coast and left to drift. Eventually, it sank, possibly because of a Russian torpedo. Rescue boats were not sent until the following day. Only one passenger survived.

18
Reprieve

Dr. Schwarz pushed the paper across the desk toward us and pointed at the line on which we were to sign. Hand shaking, I picked up the pen and scrawled *Ida Piller*, then offered the pen to Maurice.

Santo Domingo! We had just signed away five years of our lives to work in swamps. But how much worse would it be to stay in Europe? There was no way to answer that question. Although our affidavits were still under consideration at the American consulate, the pressure to act had intensified with the departure of the refugee train back to Berlin. Would we be forced to return to Belgium or, worse, shipped to our official country of origin, Poland? I had been exchanging letters with my family during our stay in Lisbon, but they were filled with the tedium of daily living, not with news of the war. The risk of writing anything that might bring suspicion from the Germans was too great. We did know that since the Gestapo had arrived in Antwerp in November, life had become harder there and that our families and friends were now required to wear the yellow Star of David so that everyone would know they were Jews. What indignities were next? There were no answers, only questions.

Our departure to Santo Domingo was delayed. Perhaps Dr. Schwarz needed to find more people, or perhaps a ship needed to arrive to carry us away. For whatever reason, we did not leave right away.

Later that week, we were called to the American consulate.

We stood before the desk of the hated man, wondering why we had been summoned.

He looked down at a folder of papers. I could see that it was filled with letters and affidavits about us. His spoke reluctantly, as if the words tasted bitter.

—Well, it looks like your visas have come through.

—Our visas? To the United States?

—What do you think? Of course! I'm sick of all your affidavits. You've given me ten!

We could hardly believe our good fortune!

44. In desperation, we signed up to drain the swamps in the Dominican Republic.

—Of course, you have to wait for a visa number.
Our hearts sank a little.
—How long...?
—How do I know? Now, get out of here!

* * *

Our anxiety mounted as the weeks passed. Finally, after four weeks, we were notified that our visa number had come through. We could emigrate to the United States.

We hurried to the HIAS offices to tell them, for they would be paying for our passage. We must have danced the entire way!

Our passage on the Portuguese ship SS *Nyassa* was secured, but the ship was not scheduled to be in port for another week. Our enthusiasm was dampened. We again thought of the *St. Louis*, turned away from Cuba, and of the train from Berlin, sent back for want of a few days' extension on the visas.

Then a letter arrived from the American consulate.

I ripped it open and read. It requested that we return to the consulate, but it gave no reason.

—No! We can't!
—They'll take our visas away!
—I won't go. I absolutely will not go!

We were too terrified to do as the letter bid. We asked other refugees, but no one else had received a letter. Every emotion that can be imagined raced through our hearts. For the next week, until the SS *Nyassa* arrived, we hid in our room in the refugee center, venturing out only for food. We were taking no chances!

Finally, on June 3, 1941, two days before my twenty-second birthday, we walked up the metal gangway and into steerage, the third-class section in the bottom of the boat.

We did not know whether we would be turned away when we reached the United States or sent on some hopeless journey from one country to another.

For over a year, we had been searching for a country that would welcome us, harbor us from the hatred raining down on

45. We left for New York on the SS Nyassa.

Jews all over Europe. We could not know whether the United States, too, would close its doors.

The journey across the Atlantic took ten days, and I was terribly seasick the whole way. In steerage, the men and women were segregated, with 200 women crammed together. It was too much for me. I found a deck chair on a second-class terrace and collapsed next to a woman who was also avoiding steerage. We spent our days and nights there, becoming good friends as we rode out the pitching, heaving voyage. She too, was relatively newly married, and our husbands vied with each other to bring their "brides" oranges and other goodies.

On the night of June 13th, the ship huffed into the New York harbor. The city twinkled against a velvet sky. Our hearts raced with anxiety. We still had no way of knowing if we would be allowed to stay. Because the ship had arrived at night, no one was allowed to disembark until the next day.

On June 14th, Maurice's birthday, we stepped onto American soil. Our hands shook as we handed the agent our visas. But we had nothing to fear. The papers were handed back to us, and we were nodded on our way.

Around us, the city bustled with the normal business of a place that had not tasted the horrors of war. Everything looked new compared to the cities of Europe we had grown up in.

Maurice took my hand, which had finally stopped trembling.

—You know, Ida, today, we are starting fresh. We will be living in America now, so I think I should have an American name. At home I was Moishe. To my friends in Belgium I was Maurice. Now I will be Morris—Morris Piller. What do you think? A new name for a new life.

I looked up into my husband's handsome face. Through most of our journey, Maurice had remained resolutely optimistic. His cheerfulness had kept my spirits up and our eyes on the prize of freedom. Our future was still uncertain, but I knew that whatever happened, we would face our problems as we had begun them—together.

Afterword

For some readers, this is a story of adventure and daring. To Ida Piller-Greenspan, it is a reminder of the daily anguish she and Morris endured trying to find a country willing to open its doors to two Jewish refugees. More difficult still, it is a reminder that her parents, sister Rosa, brother-in-law Max, sister-in-law Cylia, and other family members and friends lost their lives in the whirlwind of hate that was the Holocaust.

Of the 90,000 Jews living in Belgium at the beginning of World War II, 20,000 hid and 25,000 fled. Of the rest, almost all perished in the Nazi death camps.

Of Ida and Morris's family, only Bronia, Marc, Morris' mother, Annie, and Charly survived in Belgium. After her wedding night, Ida never saw her father or sister Rosa again.

* * * *

Samuel Wetstein—Ida remembers her father as an industrious, hard worker who labored fourteen-hour days at the store to provide for his family in Antwerp. He was a progressive man, one of the few Jewish men of his generation who was clean shaven. He had sported a mustache at one time, but he shaved it off when he saw a picture of Hitler. Samuel, once the head decorator for the Austro-Hungarian Court, was deported from Antwerp and killed in Auschwitz.

Marinya Wetstein—Ida's mother was a wonderful cook who not only managed the household but also helped her husband in his store. A strong, loving woman, she stressed adherence to the Golden Rule and the importance of her children's education. Marinya was deported from Antwerp and killed in Auschwitz.

Rosa Wetstein—Ida's younger sister was thirteen on Ida and Morris' wedding night, the last time they saw her. Rosa was so loved by Ida and their older sister Annie that when Rosa was born, Ida and Annie threw away their dolls. Rosa was deported from Antwerp at age fifteen and killed in Auschwitz.

Max Szwajcer—The husband of Ida's sister Annie, Max took the advice of the *Judenrat* (a Jewish Council set up by the Nazis to serve as a local puppet government) and signed up to work in a German work camp. He was on the last such busload of workers, as it soon became apparent to the *Judenrat* and the Jewish community at large that people in these work camps were being sent on to concentration camps. He was later deported and killed in Auschwitz.

Annie and **Charly Szwajcer**—Ida's sister Annie was devastated when she found out her husband Max had been sent to Auschwitz. She decided to go into hiding but was not sure how her four-year-old son

Charly would fare in hiding. Annie's neighbor Malvinne (with whom Charly was chatting the day Annie learned about Max's fate) saw how upset Annie was and suggested that she contact Malvinne's brother Eugene and sister-in-law Anna—a childless couple living in Duerne, a suburb of Antwerp—to see if they could take care of Charly for the duration of the war. Despite the danger, Eugene and Anna agreed. Annie often peeked at Charly from behind the farmhouse, but to ensure his and his guardians' safety, Charly did not see his mother for four years and had to pretend Anna was his mother. Annie went into hiding and spent her days away from her apartment, pretending to be employed so her neighbors would not suspect she was in hiding. She moved whenever she sensed people were becoming suspicious. Both Annie and Charly survived. After the war and the death of her husband Max, Annie married **François Bransdorfer**, a friend of Morris's (whom Morris and Ida had run into in Toulouse).

Bronia, Marc, Cylia, and **Leon** and **Rudel Piller** went into hiding together during the war.

Bronia Piller—Before Belgium was attacked, Morris's sister Bronia ran summer camps for children. During the war, in addition to participating in the Belgian Resistance, she managed a small orphanage of about twenty Jewish children. One day German soldiers came to the orphanage demanding to see her. The staff pretended she was not in. The soldiers ordered them to tell Bronia to get the children ready for travel the next morning. That night, Bronia placed all the children with farmers and neighboring families, and she took one of the girls, Edith, with her. (She later adopted Edith.) When the Germans returned the next day, the orphanage was deserted.

Marc Eisenmann—Morris's nephew Marc, just fourteen when the war began, played an important role in the Belgian Resistance, running raids on German soldiers, publishing and distributing an underground newspaper, and participating in many subversive activities. He lived in fear until an encounter with an SS officer who had just killed his girlfriend in a raid. It ended in a knife fight, and he stabbed the officer to death. He then panicked and ran. As a result of this incident, he was convinced that he would not survive the war, and he felt the weight of fear drop away. He grew to think of himself as a *hunter* rather than as hunted. At the end of the war, he was surprised to find himself alive. At the age of twenty, he married his seventeen-year-old girlfriend Jackie, and they emigrated to the United States in 1947 with his mother Bronia, adopted sister Edith, and grandmother Rudel.

Leon and **Rudel Piller**—Morris's parents were both in their seventies when the war broke out. Morris's father Leon was a deeply religious but pragmatic man. He died of a heart attack while in hiding. Morris's mother Rudel survived and came to the United States after the war. She died in her eighties in New York City.

Cylia Piller—Morris's sister served as a courier for the Belgian Resistance. One day, as her family watched in horror from the window, they saw her walk by followed by two German officers. She must have been aware that the officers were behind her, for she walked past the apartment without looking at it. Her family never saw her again. Later they learned she had been deported to Auschwitz and killed there.

Afterword

Paula and **Rachel**—Two of Ida's three closest friends, Rachel (middle in photo) and Paula (bottom in photo), were invited to Ida and Morris's wedding and reception. (Ida is at the top in the photo.) Rachel had enough money to leave Europe, but as she was born in England and was therefore a British citizen, her British passport was not safe to use (since Germany was at war with England). Paula did not have sufficient funds to leave the country, but she had a Polish passport. Paula gave Rachel her passport, and the photograph was changed. Rachel bought a visa to Cuba for $3,000 and from there managed to get to the United States. Paula was deported from Antwerp and killed in Auschwitz.

Anna was the third of Ida's closest friends. She could not come to the wedding because at the time, she was having cosmetic surgery on her nose. When the Germans invaded, the Red Cross evacuated all hospital patients and their families to England, so Anna and her family survived.

Index

American Jewish Joint Distribution Committee, 139, 144
Antwerp
    after the Germans invade, 11
    heading back to, from La Panne, 59–62
    leaving, 78
    wedding in, 3

Barcelona
    arriving in, 133
    traveling from, to Madrid, 135
Berlin, train from, 149–151
Blitzkrieg, 14, 40
Bordeaux
    French Government in, 91
    traveling from, to Pau, 97
    traveling to, 95
British Expeditionary Force, 40, 56
Brussels
    picking up Bronia and Marc, 17
    spending wedding night, 7
    traveling from, to Courtrai, 22–31

Cirque de Gavarnie
    crossing Pyrenees near, 106
    surveying, 99
Courtrai
    arriving in, after 48 hours in a train, 31
    buying tickets to, 22
    traveling from, to La Panne, 45
Cuba
    allowing refugees with money, 144
    turning away SS *St. Louis*, 59

Dominican Republic, 144, 157
Dunkirk, heading toward, 40, 45

English Channel, 45, 56

Family and friends
    Anna (Ida's friend), 167
    Bransdorfer, François (Maurice's friend), 117
    Eisenmann, Marc (Bronia's son), 3, 166
        in Brussels, 8, 11, 17, 21
        in La Panne, 48
        on the train to Courtrai, 22–24, 27
        returning to Antwerp, 60
    Paula (Ida's friend), 3, 167
    Piller, Bronia (Maurice's sister), 3, 11, 13, 37, 165
        in Brussels, 17, 21
        in La Panne, 48
        on the train to Courtrai, 22, 27
        returning to Antwerp, 60
        talking with Ida's parents regarding Maurice, 69
    Piller, Cylia (Maurice's sister), 3, 13, 60, 69, 166
    Piller, Leon (Maurice's father), 3, 13, 37, 69, 166
        on the train to Courtrai, 22
        opposing Ida and Maurice's plan to leave, 78
        returning to Antwerp, 60
    Piller, Rudel (Maurice's mother), 3, 13, 37, 166
        on the train to Courtrai, 22, 27
        opposing Ida and Maurice's plan to leave, 78
        returning to Antwerp, 60
    Rachel (Ida's friend), 3, 167
    Szwajcer, Annie (Ida's older sister) 3, 63, 78, 89, 164–165

Szwajcer, Charly (Max and Annie's son), 3, 63, 78, 89, 164–165
Szwajcer, Max (Annie's husband) 3, 63, 78, 89, 164
Wetstein, Marinya (Ida's mother), 3, 73, 77–78, 164
Wetstein, Rosa (Ida's younger sister), 3, 63, 78, 164
Wetstein, Samuel (Ida's father), 3, 77, 163
Franco, 95, 110
Franklin D. Roosevelt, 59

Gavarnie, 99, 105
Ghent, 62
Gurs, French concentration camp in, 89, 91, 117

Hebrew Immigration Aid Society (HIAS), 139, 149, 159
HIAS, *See* Hebrew Immigration Aid Society
Hitler, 70, 91, 153
   and Franco, 95, 110
   halting attack on Dunkirk and La Panne, 48, 56
   launching *Blitzkrieg*, 14
Hitchhiking with German military trucks, 80–83
Hotel *Sholem Aleykhem*, 133

Istanbul, Struma sinking near, 153

Kristallnacht, 70

La Panne
   arriving in, 45
   bombed in, 48
   German soldiers in, 55
   heading toward, 40, 45
   leaving, 59
Le Perthus
   arriving in, 127
   traveling from, to Barcelona, 133
Lisbon
   arriving in, 139
   traveling from, to New York, 159
   trying to get visas in, 141–145
   U.S. consul in, 143, 145, 157
Long, Breckenridge, 153
Lourdes
   arriving in, after crossing the Pyrenees, 115
   arriving in, from Pau, 99
   traveling from, to Toulouse, 115

Madrid, 135
Maginot Line, 8, 14
Marseilles
   traveling from, to Perpignan, 127
   traveling to, 119, 123
   trying to get visas in, 125
Menin
   arriving in, 39
   unable to cross the border at, 40

New York, arriving in, 161

Ostend, missing the connecting train to, 7

Paper wall, 153
Paris
   arriving in, 87
   touring, 89
   traveling from, to Bordeaux, 95
   Wetstein family experiences in, 77
Pau
   arriving in, 99
   traveling from, to Lourdes, 99
   traveling to, 95–97

Perpignan, 127
Porto, 139, American consul in, 143
Pyrenees, crossing, 105–108

Red Cross
   in Courtrai, 31
   emptying Wetstein apartment and store, 66
   in Paris, 77, 87
Romania, Struma from, 153
Royal Air Force, 56

SS *Nyassa,* boarding, 159
SS *St. Louis,* 59
San Nicolas de Bujaruelo, arriving in, 109
Santo Domingo, *See* Dominican Republic
Spain
   agreement with Germany, 110
   crossing into at Le Perthus, 128
   crossing Pyrenees into, 108
St. Cyprien, French concentration camp in, 91, 117, 125
Struma, 153

Toulouse
   arriving in, 115
   traveling from, to Marseilles, 123
Turkey, Struma sinking near, 153

U.S. Consul
   in Lisbon, 143, 145, 157
   in Porto, 143

Vichy Government, 91, 95
Vienna, Wetstein family's life in, 77

About the Author and Writer

Author **Ida Piller-Greenspan** grew up in Antwerp, Belgium, where she attended the Academy of Fine Arts. World War II interrupted her studies. On their wedding night, she and her husband fled from the Nazis. After the long ordeal that is documented in this book and in her pictorial diary, they arrived in New York and settled there. Most of the members of her family were deported and perished in Auschwitz.

While raising two children and helping with the family business, Piller-Greenspan continued her art studies in New York. She attended the Art Students' League and studied with Isaac Soyer at the Brooklyn Museum Art School. She received her Bachelor of Arts in Fine Arts from Queens College on her sixtieth birthday. She has lectured on the history of art, printmaking, and sculpture, and she has taught courses in painting and ceramics. In addition to printmaking, she has worked in oil, watercolor, pastel, charcoal, and acrylic.

Throughout her career, Piller-Greenspan has had numerous exhibits in the United States and abroad, including:
- Ghetto Fighters' Museum (Asherat, Israel). Her work is part of their permanent collection.
- American Gathering of Jewish Holocaust Survivors (Washington, D.C.)
- Paul Klapper Art Center, Queens College (Flushing, N.Y.)
- Jewish Federation of Greater Dayton (Dayton, Ohio)

Piller-Greenspan has garnered numerous awards, and her art has been shown in many juried and invitational group shows, including:
- Cork Gallery at Lincoln Center (New York, N.Y.)
- Jacob Fanning Gallery (Wellington, M.A.)

- UNESCO Slide Exhibit (Germany)
- Queensborough Art Society (Queens, N.Y.)

Her work has appeared in many art publications and reviews, including a close-up in *Newsday* and a special mention in the Gallery Guide of *Artspeak*, where she is described as a master of minimal-color field art. In 1997, Piller-Greenspan was interviewed and videotaped by members of Steven Spielberg's Visual History Foundation: Survivors of the Shoah. Her interview is part of the library of testimonials stored by that organization.

Piller-Greenspan currently lives in Boulder, Colorado, where she continues to exhibit her work and tell the story behind the pictures.

Professional writer **Susan M. Branting** was selected by Ida Piller-Greenspan and her daughter Rosie Piller to bring her story to life. Piller-Greenspan wants to reach as broad an audience as possible, in a manner that will illuminate the context in which she and her husband acted and the specific circumstances in which they found themselves.

Ms. Branting holds a master's degree in Journalism and has more than twenty-five years of experience writing and editing for newspapers, magazines, public relations, and a variety of other areas. Through interviews with Piller-Greenspan as well as an examination of written material and historical information, Branting has created a tense narrative that captures not only the events of Piller-Greenspan's experiences but also the depth of the terror and confusion she and her husband endured.

For Product Safety Concerns and Information please contact our EU representative GPSR@taylorandfrancis.com
Taylor & Francis Verlag GmbH, Kaufingerstraße 24, 80331 München, Germany

www.ingramcontent.com/pod-product-compliance
Lightning Source LLC
Chambersburg PA
CBHW081816300426
44116CB00014B/2381